MAN BEING

Volume I: *The Transmission*

MAN BEING

Volume I: *The Transmission*

Communicated to
Dramos & Bohemias

ISBN 978-1-9991777-0-6

This book is not a religious or spiritual treatise. It contains truths about Man Being's origins and about your options to exist free of form. It addresses what exists beyond "death" and beyond the Earth plane reality. This is the beginning of your understanding that reincarnation is not immortality and that the World of Immortality awaits you all.

TABLE OF CONTENTS

Prologue

Introduction

1

Believers and Unbelievers

What questions will the Reader have while reading this book?

There will of course be a question about our existence and our world including a concern of why we are not widely known, from where your experience has developed and why there is not more experience with the communication in our world. There is a succinct belief that you can only accommodate that which you see. Belief is based on experience that you can also relate to your own experience. The experiences you term "supernatural" or "out of this world" are harder to explain.

How can we overcome that?

You will have a difficult time explaining this to those readers that do not subscribe to other possible existences. The Reader will inevitably ask, "How do I know this exists and how do we know this is the development of a truth that we would like to acquire?" There is a correspondence between those that are willing to explore this understanding further and those that already have questions about their existence. There is disrepair in your awareness and some of you will feel more inclined than others. This is the meaningful coincidence you will establish with your readership. There must be a meaningful coincidence so that there is also an emotional correspondence to the discussion. If one's beliefs are based on an emotional connection there is a highly proven occurrence that you will be able to reach an understanding despite any initial doubt.

Are you saying that the book is just for believers?

There is an opportunity for you to attract the attention of both types of candidates in your readership. The readership will primarily be those who are interested and also those who are now curious. The curiosity will not be based on the title or premise of your book. There will be a public interest in this area that will allow readers to explore the dissemination further. The book will coincide with a popular change in belief. The timing of the release of the book will coincide with a popular experience. This experience is in a jurisdiction that will allow you to significantly respond to those who are identified as "unbelievers".

Can a dialogue of this nature sway an unbeliever?

The chances that you are persuading the unbelievers to explore further are higher when there is a general awareness. It is a matter of timing. It will attract some unbelievers. There will be a small percentage of unbelievers who are converting their beliefs and opening up the possibilities but there will soon be a reconciliation that will allow a repair in the general belief.

What is the goal of this dialogue?

You will want to experience the release of your Light Body. You are not the body form that you currently exist in. The Light Body in full repair is an assembly in shapes and sounds that are given to you in a frequency that is contained in this

3

dialogue. You can absorb the codes in this communication. The ability for you to be a fluid Light Being is contained in this dialogue stream. There are codes that you are receiving that will reawaken the remembrance of your Being and remembrance of your fluid Light Being. We will discuss the Lemuria state, which is a remembrance of the fluid Light Body movement. The continuous information that you are reassembling in this dialogue will enable you to heal your Light Body. The repair of the Light Body is the project that you are involved in.

The information contained in this book was revealed over the course of a year. Will it have the same impact on the Reader?

What you are asking for cannot be measured. The Beings that read and absorb the information contained in this book will each have a different experience. The level of experience depends on the previous level of experience in a previous incarnation of experience. Those Beings who have not encountered this level of commitment with our experience and commitment of awareness will experience a different level of awareness. The book is available for all. There is no condition as a prerequisite reading or teaching. There is information in this book that will trigger a reconnective experience for all. The level of the commitment is an individual experience. Those that choose to reassemble their Light Body and reassemble their beliefs in the existence of the Light Body will continue their journey.

2

The Transmission

We have been told that the "Light Body" is our true existence. Why then does the Soul or Light Body enter a physical reality? Why leave a heightened state for a restricted one?

> There is a program designed to lure you. Currently, you are sent here enslaved. You are a dominion of slaves. You cannot think or speak or do anything beyond what you have been programmed for. You think you are far ahead yet your accomplishments and achievements are not unique.

Why can't we see you or always hear you?

> You don't understand the process. The process was given to you but you no longer follow it. It has been taken away from you for now.

What has been taken away?

> The knowledge.

Who is deciding this?

> Your lack of gateway allowance is a mistreatment of Man Being. The allowance and the source of your frustration will be corrected soon. You cannot have the knowledge until we achieve the transmission. The transmission will once again enable gateway allowance.

What is the transmission?

> It is a rescue mission to modify your awareness. If there is awareness then those who understand the change will accept the modification. The

6

modification will be sent via the transmission. The transmission will be sent via cells. If you choose to be a part of this then your modification will assist in the acceptance of the transmission.

How can a person ask for modification? Can we ask for it?

How can you ask for something that you do not understand? First, you must undertake to understand. This dialogue is an exchange of code and information that will assist you in understanding what you require.

Do we have to understand quantum physics to be modified or can we accept that there is something we don't understand and want the modification?

If you can avoid the plan to want everything now, the disorder will be adjusted accordingly. What you need to insist upon is acceptance that things must change to benefit all.

If our heart beats without us telling it to beat why doesn't the mind also automatically adhere to the "greater good" principle?

Does it though? Does your heart function in an isolated matrix? Does it function unaware, uninhibited by your decision-making? What do you think occurs when input is suggested and you manoeuvre to repair your thoughts? What I am trying to achieve with you is not to explain how everything works but how everything is. This is a different solution.

7

What exactly are humans lacking genetically that will take form after the "transmission"?

> A chromosome repair. Modification and repair will occur on a point of the DNA strand. Proprioception.

Proprioception?

> This is how you are functioning – proprioception. You will not need to know where you are going once modified. In proprioception you go or you grow where you are told. You are directed. This linear imbalance is what we would like to correct.

How exactly will our bodies function with this correction/modification?

> There will be no bodies. You will have no form. The modification that we will be undertaking with you is with the 12th to 13th DNA strand. This has been cut off and regulated so that you cannot understand or allow a change in form that will permit a time travel condition.

We can time travel? How will that shape our world?

> You will achieve self-governance once and for all. The situation as it stands today is not desirable as Man Being is pulled in many different directions and axes of guidance. Our modification will override exponentially. If you believe that sound is resonance and the correction that we seek to achieve

is modified in these circumstances then the correction will be a positive one. Our modification will enhance a string of information that needs to resonate in the cells.

Are there any Beings in the Earth plane who already have these modifications?

Please refer to those animals in the sea that presently have these abilities. You are familiar with the Octopus but not enough with those sea creatures that are at great depth. They have been and are being watched and researched. What you don't understand is the benefit. What you don't see are the benefits of cellular exchange. When we achieve the meaning behind the cellular exchange then you will see a monumental shift – what you presently call a paradigm shift.

Have past civilizations achieved this knowledge and transmission?

Yes. Do you believe that this is something that is achievable?

Yes, but the Earth's population is controlled by powerful organizations that discourage freethinking.

This is not something that can be agreed upon in consultation with Earth's "powerful organizations".

Who is not allowing humans to have access to knowledge or to the "gateway" as you put it?

There have been repeated rescue missions or "Repair Projects". You will learn of allegiances and agendas that are not benevolent to your cause. The truth of the matter is that Man Being is the primary cause of the obstruction. Man Being can choose to ascend. You must shift your beliefs. You are contained in a grid pattern. You will gain further knowledge as the dialogue continues.

Are we the only species that is currently stuck in a "grid pattern"?

You are the only kind stuck in this way. This dilemma is unique.

Is it unique in our galaxy or unique across the universe?

It is unique. There is nothing like this going on anywhere.

How did humans get to this point?

When Man Being split, when you directed yourselves elsewhere, you abandoned the responsibility to change. You abandoned the responsibility. You aborted the mission.

What do you mean when you say Man Being "split"?

The repair experience is the "homeward" journey. Each of you is part of a soul ascension group. The understanding that there is a choice and a choice to remember the connections is what defines you singularly in this experience of ascension.

What is the choice?

> It is ascension. It is coming home. The choice is to voluntarily disconnect and reassemble your Light Body. Some of you have made the choice. Others have not.

What does it mean to "voluntarily disconnect"?

> Many of you are experiencing "death" as an involuntary disconnect. When we use the term "voluntary disconnect" we are bringing awareness to your ability to reassemble your Light Body. Man Being is not required to choose or endure the "death experience".

The term "voluntary disconnect" sounds like it can be interpreted as suicide. Are you recommending suicide?

> This is precisely what we are not recommending. The suicide construct is not a template for awareness. There is no correlation between the two. Your readership will learn more of the voluntary disconnect in this book. This is not a recommendation to take your own life. We will correct this misunderstanding as we proceed in this dialogue.

What occurs if we don't choose to voluntarily disconnect or ascend?

> What occurs is the perpetuation of the reincarnation state. Karmic experiences are not allowing Man Being to repair. Choosing a new incarnation does not benefit the ascension growth. The choice before

you is equivalent to going home versus being stuck in a limbo state. Reincarnation is not ascension.

Would you say that we've romanticized reincarnation to our own detriment?

> This is an accurate assessment. If you want to experience a world that is equivalent to what you are referring to as "Heaven" you must choose to disconnect. You must choose to believe that the reincarnation loop is not awareness. It is an ideology that limits your existence. The choice to make the disconnect experience is what is hampering Man Being's ability to fulfill the completion of the repair and experience.

We are not familiar with the "disconnect" as an afterlife option.

> There is a fulfillment and a prophecy that is remembered when the reconnections are completed and the disconnect experience is made.

Is an understanding of the voluntary disconnect the first phase of Man Being's repair?

> We believe that if you understand then you will choose to return home and reassemble. We need an allowance to bring the matter to a conclusion. We cannot make the changes fast enough for your liking because the gateway has been obstructed. You use things for your benefit and do not see the harm that this does. This lack of understanding makes for a difficult situation as you block your own entryway. If you do continue to align and allow some

modification there could be a repercussion of change.

What is the "prophecy" you refer to?

A prophecy to annihilate awareness. Access denied. The prophecy began when time began as you regard this now. You, Man Being, were no longer permitted or guaranteed an assured gateway. What has developed and what you consider your oral history is not the truth. If you realign your "thinking" you will soon believe that we have set things on their course and the obstruction for Man Being will no longer be deemed the normal manifestation of your reality. Momentum begins when you ask the question: What decision do I need to make now?

Why were we no longer guaranteed an assured gateway?

Man Being would not allow a discussion of terms. The allowance was traded in discourse accordingly. The unfair "reality" was no further allowance. When you no longer have control of a gateway you no longer have access to help. This help could no longer be achievable when the gateway was closed. When Man Being chose to split it divided alliances. This is a matter that we will revisit.

You say that humans use things for their benefit that obstruct the gateway. Please give us an example.

The Man Being condition is consumption. You destroy. You choose not to rebuild. You choose not

13

to adjust your "thinking". Your condition of
consumptive awareness will not align.

Please expand on "consumptive awareness".

The consumptive madness that you guarantee in
your "lifetime" is apprehensible. Your purpose now
is to make a decision and commit. If your
considerable efforts are benevolent you will soon see
a shift that will allow you to express your
questioning accordingly.

What is the commitment?

Man Being must choose to commit to the
modification. You will receive instructions if the
commitment is made and they will be relayed soon
after we complete an. introductory reception
adjustment. You cannot retrieve the information
until you are aware that it exists.

Please elaborate on what you mean by "soul ascension
group"?

There is a decision that you are making to reconnect
with those Beings you are referring to as your "loved
ones". This is a correct assembly of the soul
ascension group experience and will further you
toward the decision to proceed through the gateway
to the homeward experience.

Has this "homeward experience" been described in our
documented history or religious scripture?

You will be frustrated in your attempts to identify the descriptions as they have all been revised to steer you away from the truth. You can refer to the homeward experience as the "Iridis Gateway". We will give you an example of how Iridis has been alluded to in popular mythology.

Is "Iridis" a Being or a gateway?

The voluntary disconnect experience requires that the assembly of your soul group makes the journey through the Iridis Gateway experience and makes the reconnection with the world that you are designed to exist in. This is the achievement of the Lemuria state.

NOTE: "Lemuria" is a hypothesized lost land or sunken continent from ancient times. Some theories state that it extended across the Pacific Ocean. Lemuria's existence has not been proven.

What more can you tell us about the Iridis Gateway experience?

Please describe Dramos' vision of the tall white Being for your readers and we will continue this discussion.

3

What Is
I R I D I S?

DRAMOS' VISION: "I woke up suddenly to a strange sound. I could hear assisted breathing through an apparatus as though it was submerged. Someone was on the stairs. A tall white Being was silently communicating with me. It was here to retrieve me. I said in my mind, 'not now, please go away'. I was frozen. I had no idea that someone would actually make a visitation."

Is the Being in Dramos' vision what you're calling "Iridis"?

> The Being that you have experienced has modified and made a connection between our world and your world. The Being you have described in your experience is a Messenger. Iridis is not the Being. Iridis is the gateway that both you and the Messenger Being are experiencing with us. Your understanding that someone has visited you is correct and your understanding that you are visiting our world is also a correct belief. Please believe that you are connecting with our world and there is a manifestation of your Being in our world. It is working both ways.

Is the term Iridis an acronym? Why are you calling it Iridis?

> The Iridis experience is constructed in a 6-part journey. **The Iridis construct is an ability to reconnect and make the connection between our worlds.** The connection and in your case the reconnection of experience is the reconnection of the experience of our worlds. This reconnection is equated to the time travel experience.

17

What particular message is the Being delivering?

> We have discussed the voluntary disconnect principle. This is also the immortality principle. Your mythologies refer to the "Emerald Tablet" that you are attributing to the Being known as "Thoth". Messenger Beings use the Iridis experience to disseminate the "Emerald Tablet" information.

NOTE: The legend of an Emerald Tablet containing knowledge of the base of all matter and the principle of Immortality is attributed to Thoth, the Egyptian God of knowledge and wisdom.

Are you saying that the tall white Being is simply delivering information?

> This is a correct understanding. There are Messengers that are required to disseminate this information. They are involved in a voluntary undertaking to disseminate the light codes that are contained in the Emerald Tablet dissemination.

What exactly is the Emerald Tablet?

> The Emerald Tablet is an assembly of light codes. The words "Emerald Tablet" are not exactly the correct description but it is the description that you are uniformly aware of. The understanding that the symbols and the message have been contained on a material that is emerald in color and in quality is an allegory. There is a belief in this depiction, which is an appropriate tool to allow the interest to continue. Its light codes convey the ability to absorb the

18

frequency of light and to practice alchemy. These are the goals.

You mentioned that the Iridis concept is contained in a biblical context. Where can we reference this?

> The Iridis principle is revealed in the story of how the Virgin Mary has come to conceive the Being you are referring to as Jesus. The Virgin Mary is more appropriately understood as a description of the Iridis gateway. Jesus is perceived to have travelled and arrived through a womb that has been sanctified by God. The "Virgin Mary" has been created to assemble a belief in a human family unit.

Jesus was given a fictional Mother to conceal knowledge of the Iridis gateway. Is that an accurate understanding?

> The belief that the Virgin Mary is a bonafide Human Being is an incorrect understanding. The appearance of Jesus and the arrival of this Being is not connected to a human birth.

This is a significant revelation.

> This is not a principle that is widely known or will be widely accepted. Please refer to this in a careful consideration as you are confronting a belief that is monumental and inaccurate. Jesus is a Messenger that has used the gateway and the Iridis principle. Virgin Mary is best understood as an experience and a gateway experience.

Are there other figures in the Jesus story we need to redefine?

The principle Beings in the New Testament Bible dissemination are a description of those Beings who have modified and chosen the immortality and voluntary disconnect experience. There will be further discussion about the Jesus Being. Please absorb this discussion for now.

Will religious organizations – once again – hijack the Iridis information in this book?

Iridis is not designed to be contained in a religious practice or faction. It does not have an affiliation or allegiance with a specific spiritual or religious belief system or practice. The neutrality of this belief is such that it is available for all. The understanding and full practice of the Iridis experience will allow the ascension experience to be available en masse without the obstruction of religious, government or political factions. The neutrality of the new paradigm of ascension is such that religious beliefs will no longer control the gateway experience.

Will the Reader experience the tall white Messenger Being just as we have?

The experience will be similar, as the principles do not change. No two experiences are the same, however. Your readers need not be frightened by what is being discussed. Your concern that this information is somewhat of a confusing and questionable belief stream is understandable. Those of you who are prepared to make the modification will be more welcoming of the information. The concern that this is presented in an unusual way that may convey itself as a fictional tale is not something we can necessarily avoid. What is required is a willingness to continue and to absorb the information. Clarity follows modification.

4

Lemuria

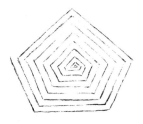

You stated earlier that the reconnection with the world that we are designed to exist in is the achievement of the "Lemuria state". Are you saying that Lemuria is an experience and not a "lost land"?

> Those who are referring to Lemuria as a geographical location and an historical event are incorrect in their description. The analogy of a location or a country is not an accurate belief. Lemuria is a state of awareness and a preparation to contain the control of the Light State Being for further modification and time travel experience. The Lemuria existence is the first step in containing the light experience. Those that are willing to acquire and experience the paradigm shift will be experiencing the Lemuria shift. This shift is an ability to acquire and further acquire the light code dynamic that allows the time travel experience. Lemuria is the first phase of the time travel experience.

You are redefining the Lemuria understanding.

> Please remember that this dissemination will not be registered for everybody and those who are prepared to absorb it will benefit. We are not requiring you to convert everyone to our beliefs and this pattern of existence, for not everybody is aligned with the Light in a similar capacity.

How can that be?

> There are many worlds of origin. If this discussion does not register with your Reader it is indicating a

different designation of alliance or world of existence.

We can all ascend but we don't all ascend to the same place or world. Is that accurate?

> This is a correct understanding. There are many worlds of origin to return to once Man Being reassembles the Light Body. We recommend that your readers do not focus on these worlds in this dialogue, as this is not absorbable at your current rate of understanding. This will be revisited in a further dialogue.

To clarify one last time – Lemuria is not an ancient land mass. Is that correct?

> Lemuria is a process. It is not a geographical boundary. It is a state, as you have a liquid state and an air state. It is a state of matter. When you begin to reformat your belief and understanding you will be able to see and fully concentrate your energy and experience the Lemuria understanding and state of understanding. Please contemplate these ideas. There is proof in this explanation.

Have humans always had the Lemuria option?

> The Lemuria existence and phase of Being has always been available for Mankind. There have been Beings who had encountered this state and have continued their journey from this state. There has been a place and a space where Beings on a massive scale were in connection with the Lemuria state. Many of you have made the journey and have

continued to make your journey. Many of you were not able to continue the journey as there has been significant interruption in the energy fields contained in your Earth density existence. Asking, "where is Lemuria" and "what happened to Lemuria" is not a correct line of questioning. The correct question is: Why has Man Being lost connection with the Lemuria state?

Is it simply a matter of knowing and tuning in?

The Lemuria state has not changed and will not change. Your contact with the World of Lyra is the entrance to the Lemuria state. The Elohim and the Angels also have the ability to communicate and experience the Lemuria state. We will return to the discussion of Lyra. For now understand that Lyra is an Intermediary World of Light in which you assemble your Light Body.

NOTE: The "Elohim" are understood to be intermediate beings between God and Man (akin to Angels), although the term has traditionally been translated as "God" or "Gods" in the Hebrew Bible.

Why would Elohim or Angels need to experience the Lemuria state? Aren't they already Light Beings?

It is an exchange of an experience. Elohim do not need to manifest the Lemuria state as they are beyond this phase of your journey of experience.

What "phase" are humans in?

There are many of you in the Earth density existence that are not even interested in experience and enlightened awareness.

Why is that?

Your society and civilization has been created and redefined so that the Lemuria state is not something that is known about or desired. The interest of many who are able to make their way to this existence will be regarded as a threat and there will be efforts to contain this. There is an ascension experience that is now unfolding on a massive scale in the Earth density existence.

What some are calling a "Lost Continent" was in reality a civilization of people who achieved the Lemuria "state". Is that correct?

This is a correct understanding. Lemuria is an example of a successful program where there was open communication and access through the gateway. Following this experience Man Being decided not to reassemble the DNA capacity. The latency of your DNA has occurred due to the atrophy and the disuse of your light energy codes. The gateway after your Lemuria experience was closed. The passage to your worlds of origin has been closed.

Is that about to change? You said there is a massive scale experience unfolding on Earth.

The realignment of a new gateway exists now for those who are able to speak and communicate with

26

us. By speaking and communicating we are referring to those Beings who are able to recode their Light Assembly for the ascension experience.

How does one know if they are able to recode their Light Assembly?

There must be a willingness to shift your beliefs. Those that are willing to acquire and experience the paradigm shift will be experiencing the Lemuria shift. This shift is an ability to acquire and further acquire the light code dynamic that will allow and does allow the time travel experience. Lemuria is the first phase of the time travel experience. Those who are referring to Lemuria as a geographical location and an historical event are incorrect in their description. Lemuria is a state of awareness and a preparation to contain the control of the light state awareness and being for further modification and time travel experience.

What precisely was Man Being capable of during the Lemuria state that you're referencing?

In the civilization and Lemuria experience there was a place and a space for listening on a massive scale. The ability to listen and acquire frequency and signal is now being reinstated in your "current" civilization. Your ability to transmit in light and travel in light and shape and sound is also being remembered. Your ability to remember these experiences will result in a profound belief that you

27

are making a physical change. The physical change is not a physical change in your cells or your form. The physical change is the reinstatement of the light experience in our world. Believe that you are concurrently forming a Light Body in our world as you shift your understanding. In the Lemuria state you will learn and experience time travel.

5

The Bible

We'd like to discuss bible scripture.

There are many bibles.

Why is there such divide between the Judaic, Christian and Muslim beliefs, which are all rooted in the Old Testament accounts of Abraham?

NOTE: Abraham is a Patriarch figure for three major religions (Judaism, Christianity, Islam). God called on Abraham to found a new Nation, believed to be the land of Canaan – later Israel. Abraham is believed to have existed 430 years before Moses and the Exodus of the Hebrews out of Egypt (ca. 1500-1200 BC). Abraham's God is referred to as Yahweh or Jehovah.

> There are Beings who exist and are fully aware of the problem that exists and these Beings have assisted in writing some of these works in an attempt to relay information. What has occurred is the further attempt to twist any truth remaining in these stories.

What exactly is the "problem that exists" that was originally being communicated in the Bible stories?

> The "problem" is that Man Being is trapped in the Earth plane existence and wishes to return home. The original idea and intention was to disseminate using creative storytelling. This would allow ideas to be absorbed without alarming the "authorities" that were and are opposed to the ascension journey.

Are you suggesting that these religious groups are misinterpreting the stories?

The real understanding of these truths extends beyond the horizon of your existence. There is information contained in the Bible dissemination but you must reformulate the understanding. Those who are not inclined to reconnect and reassemble their beliefs will have no interest in a new belief or a new belief pattern. You cannot teach someone a new belief. They must inspire themselves to that effect.

We want to be as clear as possible in this discussion. You are saying that there are truths in the Bible but that we have not correctly interpreted them. Is that accurate?

Yes. We are not suggesting that you continue to subscribe to these Scriptures in the manner that is currently practiced by Man Being. This is about perception. There is another way to absorb the information and process the beliefs as we have explored in the discussion about Virgin Mary.

The descriptions and parables in these Bible books have been grossly misinterpreted. Notwithstanding the risks you mentioned, wouldn't it have been more effective to disseminate the unfiltered truth?

Sharing your experience with others in an "unfiltered" manner does not guarantee a similar experience for readers and listeners. The ability to reconnect and understand that there is more beyond what you see and perceive is an obstacle that you are all trying to surmount. The ability to reconnect is an ability that one must acquire themselves. The understanding that there is a necessary set of questions that one must ask in order to inspire a re-connective experience is the goal of your dialogue and dissemination. Those questions are individual.

Is this dissemination teaching others how to reconnect?

The ability to ask the right questions and ask the questions that you want and need to hear is the skill that you will be teaching others. You will want to inspire others to ask the right questions. The questions that you are asking are not necessarily the questions that others will ask. This is the challenge that you all face. This was and is the challenge faced by those Beings who disseminated the Bible truths. There is an individual path of one's ascension. This path cannot be taught in a set of instructions. Experience is not instructional.

Religious organizations have been murdering people for centuries over Scriptural beliefs. It's difficult to accept what you're saying. There had to be a better way of relaying the truth.

There is a hijack of your collective experience, a misinterpretation of experience. The belief that the Bible is a literal manual for the ascension experience is an unfortunate misunderstanding and incorrect. The codes that are presented in the Bible and Bible books are not designed to ascend you via a map of your own awareness. They are a set of codes that may inspire you to ask further questions. The ability to be truthful to oneself is a challenge in your existence. There is a need to abide by a code through the Bible as in a moral code or a moral truth. The moral truth is not the same as a code of ascension.

What is lacking most in our current interpretation of these Bible books?

> The ability to understand that there is a world beyond yours is not something that is imagined in the Bible interpretation. Mankind perceiving the Bible dissemination as a literal device and manual for spiritual awareness is an unfortunate conclusion. Mankind has subscribed to the false Heaven/Hell paradigm and not sought further understanding. The ability to perceive that there are other worlds such as ours is a unique experience. This experience requires that you reevaluate your understanding of the Bible.

Are you asking us to decode the Bible for others?

> This is not your task to decode and translate the meaning. Your task is to disseminate awareness that asking questions and seeking higher truths may unlock one's own personal understanding of these Bible Books. It is the reconnection and the ability to once again engage with the world beyond your world that is the desired outcome.

Are you suggesting that we explore hidden Bible truths in order to ascend and reconnect?

> This is not accurate. This is not a suggestion that you must all now subscribe to these Scriptural truths or religious factions. Your Bibles have not been absorbed accurately. Your Bibles have been

tampered with. Your religions have been hijacked. This is what we are communicating.

Can you give us another teaching or passage in the Bible that was hijacked or inaccurately conveyed?

> Reformulate your understanding of Abraham and the attempted sacrifice of his son.

NOTE: The cited passage is contained in Genesis, Chapter 22. God tests Abraham's devotion by asking him to sacrifice his son Isaac. Just as Abraham is about to kill his son, God asks him to sacrifice a ram instead.

Why would a benevolent god require someone to murder his or her child – or any living creature for that matter?

> The ascribed violence in this parable and the appeasement to a "god" is an example of how your Bible has been tampered with. Abraham arrived to assist Man Being in the journey homeward. The Mission to bring everyone home failed. The Mission was aborted.

Was this parable simply about a failed mission to bring us back home? Three major religions based their entire belief system on Abraham's blind obedience to a god.

> The book known as Genesis is not a coherent work.

What does the sacrifice in this parable represent?

> The idea that a sacrifice is necessary is equivalent to the voluntary disconnect experience. When you recommend that the word sacrifice is equated with

the disconnect experience you will ask yourself is it "involuntary" or "voluntary". This is the issue that you must address in this passage. The history that you are rewriting is a reorganization about the belief in disconnection.

To clarify, you're saying that sacrificing the son represents an involuntary disconnect and the fact that Abraham "aborts" the sacrifice reinforces a belief in the voluntary disconnect principle.

This is a correct understanding.

It was not written very clearly.

Sacrificing the son is an involuntary disconnect experience and the parable was to make this very clear. The truth of this written account is that the meaning and definition of ascension has been misinterpreted and no longer has any clarity. The correction of this passage pertains to the reconnection with the disconnection. You must also be aware that the visitation experiences of Abraham and Moses are a similar experience.

What do you mean by "visitation experience"?

The visitation occurs after the leader of the Mission is aware and able to relay the information that the undertaking is to commence. There is an experience that you are interpreting as a Messiah event. This event is the first step in the visitation experience. Abraham was a leader who arrived to retrieve Beings and assist in their return home.

Yet Abraham wasn't able to bring us all home.

> Correct. The Mission was aborted. These experiences and missions have occurred and continue to occur. The first in the Bible dissemination is explained through this parable of Abraham and Isaac. The second is the experience of Moses and the two tablets.

NOTE: The cited passage is found in the Book of Exodus chapter 32, verse 19. In it, Moses descends from the mountain with tablets containing God's message. He becomes angered and smashes the tablets at the foot of the mountain when he sees his people dancing around a golden calf (idol worship).

Are you referring to when Moses destroys the first set of tablets in anger?

> This is correct. The broken tablets represent the aborted Mission. The Moses parable in the Book known as Exodus is a story that points to another visitation experience. We will discuss the Sinai experience further.

Back to the passage of Abraham's sacrifice, what are we to make of the dialogue between Abraham and his god?

> These dialogues are modified to perpetuate a belief system that does not benefit Man Being. What would be accurate to insert into this parable in terms of words spoken by Abraham? "The undertaking has failed we must return home".

Is the mission of this book to help us reconnect to the worlds you're calling "home"?

The Scribe's work is to unlock the questions that you all have such as, "Is there more beyond this?" Your work is not to decode and translate bible passages. Your work is to instruct others in wanting to gain further understanding about their origin. It is the origin story that you are assembling. This is not a linear history as has been presented over and over again. This is a personal experience and a personal truth experience. You are sharing your own personal account through this dialogue. This understanding will reawaken a need for others to ask the same truth and belief stream of themselves.

We don't want this book to be misinterpreted the way the ancient bibles have. We want this to be informative and inspirational and not be viewed as a manual.

The Bible understanding that it is a manual to be abided and perceived in a literal capacity is most unfortunate. It is not a literal instruction. The violence and the disruption and the state of your civilizations due to the misinterpretation of the Bible dissemination is most unfortunate. There have been several undertakings and Scribes involved in the dissemination of your Bible books. It is an assembly of many different truths. Your dissemination will be simplified in such a way that those of you that are ready to begin to ask questions about their origin will continue to do so. You are inspiring those who are ready to make a change. The journey to ascension is an individual path. There is not a manual of instruction.

How can we overcome the challenges that the Bible Scribes faced?

The Bible as it is now assembled, has not allowed its readership to think for themselves. The Bible text has been changed and maneuvered so that those who are now digesting the material are no longer able to think for themselves and decide for themselves. You are no longer allowed or encouraged to be a freethinker by subscribing to religious factions. It is the freethinking that will allow a fluid understanding and connection with our world. Detach yourselves from these outdated and incorrect belief systems.

6

Yahweh & Sinai

You've discussed the original intention of the Bible books and Abraham's mission, but we'd like to further explore the Old Testament.

> Ask your questions.

Who or what is the god of Abraham, otherwise known as "Yahweh" or "Jehovah"?

> The irresponsible dissemination that has contributed to the root of all the problems in the Abrahamic religions is such that there is an obedience and worship of a god that is not in true existence. The god "Yahweh" is not a god that is adhering to the principles that are based in the original Abrahamic belief system. Abraham is a Being who has made the full ascension and immortality experience.

Abraham formed his Light Body and ascended. Is that what you're saying?

> Yes. You have asked what Abraham was teaching. Abraham taught these principles. These principles and teachings were and are continually available but there was and is a hijacking of information in the form of your Bibles and the Ten Commandments structure.

What "god" or experience was Abraham in contact with that was later interpreted as "Yahweh"?

> Yahweh is not the name of a god. It is a system of energetic realignment through the Light Body reassembly. There is a code in this name and the word creates a significant shift in understanding

about the principle of the gateway access. The term Iridis that you have already encountered is an equivalent name that can be synergistically aligned with the word Yahweh and the principle.

This is a case of the truth staring at us in the face and not knowing it.

Yahweh has been misinterpreted to place Man Being in a slavery condition.

You previously mentioned Sinai. Yahweh is introduced to Moses as a "burning bush" at Mount Sinai/Horeb. How much of this is allegory?

The question should not be "is this a representation?". The question should be "what is being represented?". This passage in the Book of Exodus represents the allowance to enter and exit through the gateway. This marks an occasion when Man Being was offered tools to return home. This time period marks a split that redefined the obligations of Man Being.

Yahweh in these passages appears to be demanding strict adherence to laws, not offering "tools" to return home.

This choice would explain why Yahweh is referred to as a "god". This is the manipulation we have discussed. Man Being has submitted to a Ruler that does not exist.

To clarify for the Reader, we are speaking of the Mount Sinai experience. You're saying that this was an event marking a visitation.

The Sinai passages in your Bibles point to the most recent opportunity to receive the tools for ascension. It is not a meeting between Moses and a "god" named Yahweh. Many ignored the ascension tools that were offered at this time in your linear history. There is a confusion that arises when Man Being is offered an opportunity to experience ascension and understand time travel.

"Yahweh" was not a god but a tool and an opportunity to ascend and form our Light Body. Is that a correct understanding?

Yes. The remembrance of this event is the reason why you are all driven to pray and associate yourself with the Yahweh principle. It is a memory of something that you have all lost – an aborted mission. There will be no Yahweh principle or belief once the principle of a new understanding is disseminated. Once Man Being is converted to a new understanding of their own ascension they will abandon the Yahweh principle and proceed through their own ascension enlightenment experience.

You refer to this event as a "visitation". Please describe for us what actually occurred at Mount Sinai?

The Sinai descriptions are an allegory. What they are pointing to is a "time" when we attempted to relay information about the ascension experience and the voluntary disconnect experience. The concept of Yahweh being a "god" that requires strict adherence to practices and beliefs so that you may enter into "Heaven" is incorrect. Your understanding of Yahweh and the Ten Commandments are not aligned with the original information that was shared. The information has been changed and needs to be reevaluated or decoded.

The Sinai account in the Bible was actually about ascension and immortality. Is that correct?

The Sinai account points to a choice you made. Man Being rejected the path to assemble the Light Body.

What exactly did we choose during this Sinai experience?

You chose the reincarnation stream that has and continues to be the hallmark of your religious beliefs. Religious existence is a commitment to and belief in the reincarnation cycle. The reincarnation cycle is essentially the reason you are trapped in your existence, as you have already ascertained.

The idea of reincarnation is not rooted in the Tanakh, Christian Bible or Quran. These scriptures focus on the reward and punishment of souls through what is often termed "Judgment Day".

The judgment cycle perpetuates your further reincarnation cycle. Those of you who do not have an understanding of ascension or who choose not to modify are influenced to return to the Earth plane upon the involuntary disconnect experience – or what you are calling "death".

The Abrahamic religions take the belief that if we follow a moral code we will earn good Judgment and therefore Eternal rest, aka Heaven.

> There is a belief that by being a "good individual" you may achieve the immortal state. This is not a correct belief or a correct dissemination. We are not suggesting that this gives you free reign to participate in whatever you wish and not abide by your codes and laws that have been created in your world. We are suggesting that the quality of the Light Being state and the Lemuria state is such that the principle of "good deeds" and "bad deeds" do not exist. There is a different state of existence where you do not receive understanding or an undertaking of good or bad.

What is that state of existence?

> There is a flow and a fluid movement of light and sound and being. This existence does not coexist with right or wrong or good or evil as your religious principles adhere to.

If the Sinai visitation was an opportunity to reassemble our Light Being state, then where did the Yahweh precepts come from?

> There is another gateway experience that is being relayed through the falsified Yahweh descriptions. It is not of benefit to the Light Body path.

What is that gateway experience?

44

It is one that is continually ruled and operated under the Orion DRA Allegiance. The question of "who are the Orion DRA" will be more easily absorbed when we discuss Sirius in a further dialogue. For now understand this as an allegiance of Beings that are not endeavoring to assist Man Being in ascending.

We are being trapped by these false beliefs. Is that what you're suggesting?

DRA are ensuring that Man Being is perpetually living in a cycle of fear and misunderstanding of the correct ascension principles. The "Judgment" experience and the belief in a "god" are containing Man Being in this cycle of fear.

Is this basically a program designed to enslave humans by sending them back to the Earth plane (i.e. reincarnate)?

This is correct. The decision makers in your world are also perpetuating the myth that the immortality experience is obtained through the Judgment experience.

Is "Judgment Day" avoidable?

This understanding that one must approach the Judgment state or "Judgment Day" and proceed is an incorrect pathway and one that will continue to perpetuate the cycle of your reincarnating state. Judgment is what Man Being has subscribed to. You do not have to

choose this. There is another pathway to immortality.

What are the pathways we can choose from?

> There is the Light Body reassembly experience and there is the Judgment experience. The Light Body reassembly is the ascension experience. The Judgment experience is a ruse to keep Man Being in the reincarnation stream. This is not ascension.

The understanding that "Judgment Day" is a hoax will be difficult for some to absorb.

> These principles have been disseminated before and are continuing to be disseminated in your book. These principles and choices have been disseminated by other Beings including the Beings you are calling Jesus and Akhenaten. Your religious creations are working on a principle of reward based on good behaviour and completing multiple incarnations. This is a matter of control or what you refer to as "enslavement".

NOTE: Akhenaten was an Egyptian Pharaoh who ruled for 17 years and died ca.1335 BC. He built a new capital named Amarna and upset the established religious order by introducing and enforcing the exclusive worship of the god "Aten". Pharaoh Akhenaten is thought to be either the father or uncle of King Tutankhamen – the facts are inconclusive.

We are talking about an event but what about the people who experienced this "visitation"? The Bible books describe them as "Hebrews". Who were the biblical Hebrews? There are theories that the Hyksos people (Semitic/Asiatic people who settled in the Nile Delta) were the Hebrews?

They are the ones that contain the truth.

NOTE: The Hyksos were an ethnically mixed people of mostly Semitic origin. They invaded Egypt in the 17th century BC and ruled Northern Egypt as the 15th Dynasty from ca. 1630-1523 BC.

Please elaborate.

There is a division and a split among the people you are referring to as the Hebrews.

Are you suggesting that the Hyksos came from a Hebrew split?

They are one in the same. The split and the period after the split and the continued discussion of who has the correct lineage and access will be revealed in your pursuit of understanding.

Some have also suggested that biblical figures like Abraham, Isaac (Abraham's son) and Jacob (Abraham's grandson) were Hyksos Rulers and not Shepherds, as is traditionally believed.

They were the last Beings that had full access to the tools that would allow others to continue to return home. Abraham in particular refined a mission and completed a mission that allowed many to return home, as we have already mentioned. The return home is the "Repair Project". The Pharaohs may be equated for your understanding with the "tools". The tools of the understanding were no longer passed down. This is something that is to be corrected in the new generation that is about to commence.

You're saying that these Rulers/Pharaohs were in possession of ascension knowledge. Is that correct?

This is correct. The title of "Hyksos Ruler" or "Pharaoh" signifies Beings who are in charge of communicating ascension information to those who are trapped and wish to return home. The understanding of Abraham, Isaac and Jacob as Rulers or Pharaohs, is accurate. There is some confusion however in that not every "Pharaoh" in your historical accounts fulfilled this responsibility.

Was Pharaoh Akhenaten sharing these "tools" and was his identity redefined as "Moses" in the Old Testament? Some have proposed that Akhenaten was in fact Moses.

Akhenaten achieved considerable access and created tools of awareness but he did not fulfill this on his own. There is another Being that Akhenaten has worked with who made the key decisions. The Being known as Akhenaten's wife is the Being that you must ask us about as this Being has the tools for your further exploration and understanding about Moses. Moses is related to the Akhenaten situation in that there was a fulfillment and a requirement to complete an undertaking. Moses and Akhenaten were and are part of a Cooperation and a Council. The Being who is in charge is not being discussed.

Are you speaking of Queen Nefertiti?

This is correct. Those key Beings who are of the utmost importance to resolve the present situation are not being thought of in the correct way that will allow access to the gateway through an acquired ascension experience.

What is the correct understanding of Nefertiti's role in this account of linear history?

Nefertiti is a communicator from our world of existence and has allowed the communication and the dissemination privilege to continue. It was decided that Nefertiti was to return to our world. She was to continue the journey of ascension with other Beings that were designated for the journey. The account of her death and demise is not correctly stated and the account of the Akhenaten's disappearance is not correctly stated.

What is the correct account?

Akhenaten is a Being who experienced a full ascension experience journey and voluntary disconnect. His "disappearance" was explained through "political upheaval". There was a witness to Akhenaten's ascension experience and a resulting concern that this would cause a disruption. This understanding and historical account has been buried along with the other artifacts that are contained in a location which will soon be revealed.

The name Nefertiti is Egyptian for "the beautiful one has come". If Nefertiti was from your world, does this mean Akhenaten was apprenticed to her?

This is a correct explanation. The understanding that Nefertiti was brought from an exotic place to coincide as the wife and companion of Akhenaten is somewhat of a correct description. Her teachings and her leadership and communication was involved in the dissemination of the Aten symbolism and the correction of the ideology and the religious practice of the day. The understanding that Nefertiti would be regarded as a goddess is a correct description as she is from our world and these are the descriptions that are being used in the historical place and space in your linear account.

What exactly were the tools Nefertiti imparted to Akhenaten and others?

She has been involved in an undertaking to bring those individuals back to our world that have chosen to assist with others' ascension through dissemination on Earth. The tools and the secrets that were and are being sought after are about the listening skill and the ability to listen. The ability to listen is an acquired ability and your questions about frequency and attunement to frequency are always appropriate questions. This skill is not something that you can read about. It is a skill that you must revive. It is a lost ability. It is a re-connective ability and requirement. We will return to this discussion when we speak about the Path of the Lyre.

Is that the "Path" that the biblical Hebrews ignored at Sinai? You mentioned earlier that at Mount Sinai they were offered the tools to return home.

They did not choose the Path of the Lyre. Your readership will want to know what this is referring to. There is much confusion about this Path and world. The experience of listening is an ability that has been cut off and one that we are reinstating with you. When we use this word "listen" with you, we are attributing this experience to a new belief about your existence. We recommend that you return to this discussion in your final chapter, as this will be a transition point into your second volume of dissemination.

Please summarize the Sinaitic experience for us.

Akhenaten made the ascension journey and the proof is contained in the information and principles that were revealed in the Sinaitic experience. This was and is the Cooperation with the Being Moses. The Sinaitic experience is an experience of ascension and immortality and contains the truth about the Iridis Gateway. This teaching or understanding however has been corrupted in what you now call your Bible.

Akhenaten proved ascension to be real and others including Moses continued his principles, which were described through the biblical passages about Sinai. Is this a correct understanding?

This is an accurate understanding. Akhenaten is representative of someone who followed the belief and chose to disseminate the understanding before making the voluntary disconnect journey. The Being that you are referring to as Moses represents a mission. The Sinaitic experience or event is an

51

opportunity for mass ascension. There is a Sinai event unfolding in your "lifetime" that we will soon discuss.

During which linear years did Akhenaten disseminate his understanding?

This information was disseminated in the year of the horizon of his belief. The years that you are referring to in your linear works are somewhat correct and need to be reestablished as the following: The years of his "rulership" refer to the years of the teaching and the years of "Armana" refer to the years of the dissemination. The clues that there is a written account and evidence of the dissemination have yet to be discovered. There is an opportunity for an undertaking to retrieve this information.

Is there a discovery or artifact that can corroborate this particular information?

The realization that there is not a lot of information available about Akhenaten's existence and contribution is the key reason for your participation in this Repair Project and undertaking. The decision that King Tutankhamen would assume rulership and close or destroy the books on Akhenaten mattered most to the Orion DRA allegiance. The establishment of the Orion DRA existence on your world was created after the time period of the Akhenaten reign and ascension experience. The understanding that the gateway of knowledge would be obstructed was defined in this experience.

Did the Orion DRA originate at the time of Akhenaten or from the beginning of our linear history?

> The hybridization was not at the beginning of the linear history. The Orion DRA involvement in the Akhenaten time period is a hybridization. The Beings that you are equating with the "mixed multitude" and those who were perhaps significantly involved in corrupting the belief system of the other Beings were Orion DRA hybrids. This was how the control of the masses and the obstruction of ascension tools were achieved. The Beings that are being referred to as the "mixed multitudes" were and are in fact from a hybridization of Beings that continue to exist in your current Earth density plane. They are involved in all matters of the high-level experiences and organizations in the political and governmental and religious realms.

NOTE: In the Book of Exodus Chapter 12, verse 38, it states, "A Mixed Multitude also went up with them, and very much livestock, both flocks and herds". These are believed to be a group of non-Israelites who joined the Exodus from Egypt.

It seems odd that King Tutankhamen would comply with the destruction of his father's legacy.

> The Being Tutankhamen is not in fact an offspring of Akhenaten. This Being was aligned with the Orion DRA allegiance and was put in this position to further spread the belief that ascension was not achievable or believable. This is how the beginning of the control of information in the most recent incarnation of obstruction was originated.

Where was King Tutankhamen from?

> This Being is involved strictly with the Orion DRA strain.

How was he presented to Akhenaten and Nefertiti?

> They were not present when he took over the position of Pharaoh.

Did King Tutankhamen coexist with them while Akhenaten was on the throne?

> He did not.

Yahweh, Sinai and Akhenaten are all examples of how ascension information was blocked or obstructed or destroyed. Did we just give up the fight?

> This is not entirely accurate. There was an attempt to once again overthrow the decision makers through the Messiah experience known as Jesus. What we are suggesting is that the Messiah experience is an example of the "fight" you are referring to. The Messianic attempt to overthrow the obstruction of the knowledge gateway is a continuous experience.

7

The Messiah Experience

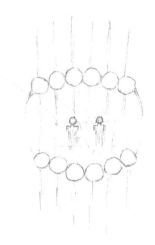

You've mentioned figures like Akhenaten, Nefertiti and Jesus but we'd also like to discuss the Being known as Thoth. He is sometimes referred to as "Humanity's greatest Teacher". Who or what is Thoth?

NOTE: Thoth is depicted as the Egyptian god of knowledge and wisdom and has been credited with the invention of geometry and medicine among other disciplines.

> Thoth is a guidance awareness system. The Thoth experience is a Messenger and Messiah experience.

It sounds like you're saying Thoth was not an actual Being.

> The understanding of a Being named "Thoth" that currently exists in your mythological accounts is somewhat of an accurate description. This is a story or experience that occurred many linear years before the disseminated accounts in the Egyptian timeline.

NOTE: Thoth mythology states that he was an Atlantean Priest King who founded Egypt after the demise of Atlantis. The myth also states that it was his knowledge that built the great Pyramid, which was used as a repository for the wisdom of Atlantis.

Thoth is the name of a Being but it also represents a guidance system for "ascension mastery". Is that accurate?

> This is an accurate understanding. To be and to experience is the same momentum. Please expand your awareness of this principle.

Can we also say that Thoth is the wisdom that a Messenger or Messiah acquires?

> This is a more accurate understanding, yes. The Thoth, Lyra and Iridis experiences are brought forth for public absorption and awareness through the Akhenaten and Jesus experiences that you are also referring to as the Messiah experience.

Thoth is believed to be the author of the Emerald Tablet, as we've already mentioned. Did Jesus and other Messengers derive their teachings from the Tablet?

> The secrets on how to navigate and enter our world are revealed in the "Tablet". These concepts and understandings have been received and continue to be received. The legacy of Jesus and the Emerald Tablet are uniquely intertwined when you consider the immortality principle. Time travel and awareness of the immortality principle is contained in the teachings of the Emerald Tablet. The Emerald Tablet existence is an organized belief that these teachings are available for those who seek to assemble the understanding. The Tablet is not a complete teaching. It is an access to the awareness and establishment of the correct belief stream.

You're equating Akhenaten with Jesus. Were they both Messiah experiences?

> The Akhenaten experience is equivalent to the Jesus experience. This is an accurate understanding.

Were Akhenaten and Jesus trying to teach people about the Thoth, Lyra, Iridis and Lemuria experiences?

These are all one in the same discussion and the very ideas that these Beings were committed to disseminating to the public. It is the Lemuria state that we wish to reactivate with you. The connection in our communication is the first step in reestablishing the Lemuria state. This is a state of awareness and a state of being that is available for all to access again. We are coinciding this dialogue stream with you in the anticipation that there will be a release of form in a permanent way. This will allow those of you who are trying to achieve the travel homeward to once again be confirmed.

Is there another historical figure, similar to Akhenaten, whose achievements haven't been properly acknowledged?

There is an equivalent experience in the incarnation with the Being that you refer to as Isaac Newton. This Being has allowed a dissemination of information that those who have studied the works may not be fully aware of. We are not suggesting that this Being is represented in a Messiah figure but there is correct information that needs to be reevaluated. There is information that has not been released correctly or disseminated correctly.

What information are you referring to?

The Being you refer to as Newton had determined a date for the arrival of a Messenger experience or what has been called "The Second Coming". These calculations were not circulated in a manner that revealed his identity or that would reach a wide readership. Please examine this material.

NOTE: Sir Isaac Newton's works were donated to the University of Cambridge upon his death in 1727. In 1936 some of these works including Newton's End of Days predictions were auctioned off in London and bought by Abraham Shalom Yahuda, a Jewish Professor and Author. Yahuda left the papers to the National Library of Israel, which received them after his death in 1951. Newton predicted the year 2060 as the coming of a new age.

Are you suggesting that his prediction was right and that there will be a Second Coming?

> The concept of a Messiah coming to alleviate the world from its misery is somewhat correct. There is a Being of a controversial nature who is manifesting in a physical form in the linear timeframe of 2034 to 2062. This public figure will once again create an upheaval that will realign your understanding of your origin.

Won't this information of a Messiah figure create more confusion? Isn't this the problem we face as a civilization – that we are always waiting for a divine figure to bring us "salvation"?

> There are Beings that make the journey as Jesus did and assist in the ascension experience. Jesus and other Beings are teachers and what you refer to as leaders and there are definitely many who have been a part of your Earth density experience already. There have been many leaders that you have effectively deified and some of these leaders you are aware of. However, the notion that a leader means "a deity" and a deity means "God" is an incorrect belief.

Why are you telling us when the "Second Coming" will arrive?

> There is a practice and belief that the suggestion of an arrival benefits Mankind in order to prepare for the ascension experience. These dates are a benefit for Man Being if you equate these dates as a state of impending preparation.

Don't we want to avoid creating a new religion around another Messiah?

> We appreciate this concern and suggest to your readers that there is no correct definition of "Second Coming" or "Messiah". Messenger Beings have continuously made visitations to assist Man Being in his ascension. Your religious practice does not serve ascension. Your deification of such Beings does not serve ascension.

How then should we perceive a Messiah figure?

> The Messiah is a monumental event. The Being that is equated with the event is not the start of the ascension experience. It is a symbolic representation of the journey of ascension. When the ascension experience occurs there are Beings who are making their way back through the gateway to reassemble members of their own soul ascension group. This will enable them to continue to integrate and form the Light Body Being that will propel them to the next world that awaits.

We're singling out individual Beings as "Saviors" when in fact the Messiah experience is a collective effort to return to our world of origin. Is that correct?

> This is correct. The Messiah experience is a collection of energies that are integrated. Holding one Being responsible for an event is an inaccuracy, but in order to explain to those who have been left behind this is a comfortable and logical device for dissemination. Those who have not made the ascension journey lack the understanding. They are not capable of fully absorbing the circumstances that are driving the ascension event and the homeward journey.

Is this why religions are so divided on who or what the Messiah is?

> The accounts of an ascension event are not always accurate as the understanding of ascension is left behind and left in the hands of those Beings who did not make the ascension experience. They are therefore limited in their full interpretation and understanding. The Beings that are equipped with the full capable understanding of the experience are no longer held in the Earth plane. Those that ascend do not remain to disseminate in writing. The understanding that Beings who have not made the full ascension experience are left to teach and share the experience is something that needs to be accounted for.

Is our history of Jesus and his message accurately documented?

There is a brief interval in the true understanding of what Jesus has brought to the teachings. The principles have been manipulated so that there is an incorrect understanding for you. This is a lack of synchronicity. The timing, the release of the information and the experience has not been aligned in a way that the public can absorb the teachings.

It seems the public isn't ever ready to absorb this type of information. You've already suggested that our DNA is corrupted.

There is no way to present information that does not frustrate those who are not ready to receive. We are asking those who function as a Messenger to contain the principles in a way that will allow Beings to absorb the ascension tools in stages. The concern about the Being known as Jesus is the accelerated way that the information was shared and continues to be shared. There is no service if information is simply disseminated without the concern that some may not be ready to fully absorb the message. Those who are not ready to absorb may need an experience that will allow them to adjust accordingly.

New Testament Scripture tells us that Jesus gave simple homilies about love, forgiveness and the Kingdom of God. It's difficult to see how people needed to absorb these concepts in stages, unless the Bible masks the true teachings. Was Jesus teaching more sophisticated ideas?

This was the unfortunate result of the Jesus legacy. This Being presented far too much information for a public that was incapable of absorbing it. There has been a profound and serious consequence of the presentation style and accelerated pattern of release of information. This is not to the benefit of Mankind to simply project and disseminate awareness without consideration of the inability for many to absorb the content. The absorption rate must be a concern. Those who wish to ascend may need guidance and may need a considerable amount of preparation in their ability to experience the teachings or information.

You mentioned that Akhenaten is connected to the Iridis experience. What is the significance of the Aten disc?

The understanding of the Aten symbolism and shape connects your understanding to the Iridis gateway announcement. The announcement and the arrival is the beginning of the intrusion.

NOTE: "Aten" means "disc" in Old Kingdom Egypt. Later during Pharaoh Akhenaten's rule it became a symbol of worship. Akhenaten is said to have enforced exclusive worship of the Aten disc during his reign.

Was Akhenaten informing people of the Iridis gateway experience?

This is correct. The worlds unite when the Aten is in full alignment with the star. The Iridis gateway allows for the reconnection to the World of Light.

What exactly is meant by the phrase "alignment with the star"?

You can no longer block the light if you are able to see and know the light.

Is the "star" a specific luminary or is it representative of all light?

> It is a representation of the light and light awareness. This is demonstrated by those Beings who are aligned with the understanding of the light of Sirius. The Aten is a code that you are aligning with your chosen belief.

NOTE: Sirius is the brightest star in our night sky. There is a detailed discussion on Sirius in Chapter 10.

Akhenaten's disc or Aten was actually a code for the gateway to immortality. Is that correct?

> There is a misunderstanding about the symbolism and a great misappropriation of Akhenaten's belief. The Aten is an understanding that there is a pathway that allows you to choose an immortal understanding of being. This understanding requires you to recreate your energy so that the time travel modality is fully connected. This is an achievement that requires a shift in your belief.

This implies that there are several belief streams.

> You can choose the immortal Lemuria state which allows the time travel experience or you can choose the reincarnation experience, which does not continue your ascension.

Akhenaten chose the immortal Lemuria state.

Akhenaten has made a choice to voluntarily disconnect and to disconnect from the responsibility in the Earth density experience. The ascension of Akhenaten is equated to the ascension in the Iridis experience. Akhenaten understood the principles of the Thoth mastery. He has mastered ascension. Mastery of ascension is assembling a disconnect experience that allows a reconnection with the world where we are assembled in.

The Book of Genesis writes that Enoch was "taken" to Heaven alive by God. Is this describing the voluntary disconnect?

NOTE: Enoch is known in the Book of Genesis as Noah's great grandfather. He is described as having walked with God throughout his lifetime and was rewarded for his devotion. He ascended into Heaven without the death experience.

Akhenaten is a similar experience to the Enoch experience. The mastery of the disconnect principle is contained in the information of the Emerald Tablet. This is not a series of symbols and instructions on how to disconnect. It is a series of experiences that coincide with a reassembly of your beliefs. To voluntarily make a disconnect there must be a mastery of your beliefs.

Which of Jesus' teachings was distorted to conceal the truth of the voluntary disconnect?

The understanding that there is a "one with god" experience is a belief that if you voluntarily make

65

this disconnect and choose the ascension experience then there is an allowance through the world that you are in a connection with.

Is that what Jesus meant when he said, "I and the Father are one"?

This is an accurate correlation. The principles that Jesus has brought to your world of existence is an example of the urgency of the disconnect principle and the urgency to incorporate this belief into your current paradigm. The principles that Jesus has mastered are contained in the Emerald Tablet. This information has been shared.

What more can you tell us about the voluntary disconnect?

The decision is an irrevocable one. There is no further choice other than the disconnect once you proceed. This disconnect is a different condition than the involuntary death experience. Voluntarily disconnecting enables you to experience time travel. The escape from the involuntary disconnect experience is a choice that you are all encouraged to make. This information is as controversial now as it was in the "time" of Jesus.

What is the true account of Jesus' message?

Jesus brought awareness that you can choose to disconnect from the reincarnation experience. The voluntary disconnect experience is the beginning of your journey and the entry into the world of allowance or what Jesus referred to as the "Kingdom of God". The resurrection experience is equivalent to the immortality principle. This principle is represented in the Emerald Tablet.

Who else has seen the Emerald Tablet?

Many before you, including the Being you are equating with Enoch, have read the Emerald Tablet. Enoch is an example of a Being who has chosen the voluntary disconnect experience. The Enoch understanding is a principle in the ascension understanding. The name "Enoch" is equated with all those who have and will make the disconnect experience.

Bible scholars and religious leaders claim to know the true meaning of their Scriptures. Are they also ascending?

The scholarly pursuit of the understanding of these Scriptures and the Emerald Tablet information will not achieve a voluntary disconnect and ascension experience. The information is a light experience. The experience of the light is the absorption of the light. The ability to absorb the meaning is also the ability to absorb the sound. There is an absorption that occurs for those of you who have made a connection with our world. The passage through our world is the passage of the voluntary disconnect.

Are you saying that the Tablet isn't a physical object?

The Emerald Tablet is not read as a book or a series of symbols to be memorized. This is an incorrect belief. This fallacy is preventing many of you from the ascension experience. We would like you to correct this understanding. The information is not physically contained on a stone Tablet. This information is brought to you in light. The Tablet is better described as a sphere and a sphere that contains the light and the light information and codes. This simplified understanding of the Emerald Tablet will allow those who are ready, to achieve an ascension experience.

The sphere containing light information can be applied to the Aten disc we've already mentioned. Did Jesus have a similar symbol or term he used that was mentioned in the New Testament?

The Eucharist and the Aten are a similar placement of beliefs. This was their belief stream.

NOTE: The Eucharist is a ceremony where bread and wine are consecrated and consumed. In the New Testament Book of John, Jesus is quoted as saying: "I am the living bread that came down out of Heaven. If anyone eats of this bread he will live forever".

Was the tall white Being that visited us delivering the light codes and light information?

This Being from your experience is a Being that has been selected to deliver the message and the responsibility of the message to you. The mission of this Being is to bring you the sphere of information.

The sphere is a common symbol in religion and artwork. Has this knowledge been hiding in plain sight?

There are many examples of well-known artworks or paintings that depict such a sphere. This will be discussed in a further dialogue.

8

Artists

You've mentioned that there are well-known works of art that depict the "sphere" or information of light awareness. Is it worth discussing how these concepts have been disseminated through artwork?

> Our world is aligned with the frequency you refer to as "artistic". What you do not realize is that the Artist is demonstrating a reconnection with our world. It is recommended that you re-examine your understanding of an artist and your own histories of such Beings.

Renaissance artists come to mind. What can you tell us about the artistic movement known as the Renaissance, which occurred between the 14th and 17th centuries AD?

> The Beings that existed in this linear time frame that you are calling the Renaissance require a re-examination, as they are part of a cooperative to disseminate information about Lyra.

The Medici Family in Medieval Florence practically bankrolled the Renaissance. Did the Medici lead a Repair Project?

NOTE: The Medici were a banking family and a political dynasty in Florence during the 15th and 16th centuries AD. Cosimo the Elder supported artists such as Donatello, Ghiberti and Brunelleschi. Cosimo's grandson Lorenzo "The Magnificent" was a poet himself and supported the likes of Leonardo Da Vinci, Michelangelo and Botticelli.

> The Medici created an alliance that continues today. Your questions involve questions about time

71

travel. Please indicate which Medici you would like to focus the dialogue on?

What can you tell us about Lorenzo de'Medici?

> This individual has mastered the ascension tools and time travel capability. He also holds knowledge of the world of Lyra and the mysteries that you are inquiring about. Florence is a reservoir of knowledge and information for you regarding artistic endeavors.

Lorenzo "mastered the ascension tools". Can you elaborate on that?

> Lorenzo is part of an undertaking to bring about a reformation in the beliefs that continue to obstruct Man Being's ascension. What is not revealed in a clear and concise dissemination is that this Being is not a Being from the Earth plane existence. Lorenzo's affiliation with the Being known as Michelangelo will further assist in understanding the events that occurred during this place and space in your linear history.

If they wanted a reformation of beliefs why were they painting and sculpting religious iconography?

> The individuals who formed an artistic alliance were also secretly involved in the overthrow of the religious information that was being disseminated at the time. Religious organizations, as you are aware, were seeking to direct Beings away from the Repair Project.

How was Michelangelo involved in the Repair Project?

> The development of the personal ties between the
> Medici family patronage and the Being known as
> Michelangelo was and continues to be a quest for
> the discovery of the truth about the existence of the
> Beings beyond the primordial realm of Lyra.
> Michelangelo is a Being who has and will continue
> to make appearances. This Being is beyond the
> Ascended Master level of experience. He has
> contained the energy of experience and the
> allowance and awareness of time travel to coincide
> with this time period in your linear account.

What specifically was Michelangelo's function in this secret
alliance of artists?

> Some of these artists, specifically Michelangelo,
> were in fact teachers for some of the Medici family
> members. The teachings and the experiences were
> shared in an oral and private dissemination so that
> the writings would not be discovered. The oral
> dissemination was also documented in artistic works,
> as this was the only way to share information
> unobstructed without the political and religious
> dangers that were surrounding this point in history.

Are the undiscovered "writings" Michelangelo's or Lorenzo's?

> Michelangelo did not limit his artistic output to one
> realm such as sculpture or painting. He involved
> himself with the writing of books that have not been
> released. There is a stockpile of his writings,
> philosophical and spiritual ideas that are contained
> in a satchel that is stored in the lower level of a

library that is affiliated with an organization in Italy. This organization is responsible for the keeping of religious works.

Do you mean the Vatican archives?

It is not a building that is affiliated with the Vatican libraries. This is the governmental building you refer to as the Pitti Palace, which also keeps and stores works that have yet to be restored and yet to be archived.

Why are these writings being concealed?

The reason why things are being stored in this way is the understanding that there is a new order in place that is waiting to take over the responsibility for these works. These works and writings are known about and they are not able to be removed or rescued from the storehouse. There is a concern that the Vatican library will obtain these works and also hoard them in their current stockpile of works.

What is the specific message in his writings?

The message and the writings in the book are specifically about the ascension experience and releasing the Light Body, similar to the voluntary disconnect. You may be asking why Michelangelo spent so much time depicting the human form. This is an indication that he would have liked you to ask the question – why is Man Being created in a way that they are perceivably very different from other Beings and very beautiful in their construct?

Bible scripture tells us we are "created in the likeness of God".

> The question of being "created in God's image" must lead to more questions about the primordial existence. Michelangelo wished to achieve the question: How is it that Man Being has come to be in such a perfect form?

His artwork seemed to be celebrating our physical form and not a "primordial existence" or "Light Body" as you put it.

> There is a misinterpretation in the meaning and intention behind his work. The work was to go beyond the physical form and not maintain the integrity of it. What we believe you will understand about the writings is that he wished to disseminate in art form the Light Body reassembly and the Light Body release. There was an unfortunate restriction on the artistic output, as the Medici family members would approve of the work of the artist before release.

Why would they disapprove if they were part of this allegiance to disseminate the truth?

> There was careful consideration to disseminate information without creating political and religious upheaval. The artists were requested to code the information so as not to upset suspecting groups who were and are opposed to the Repair Project.

What else is contained in Michelangelo's books?

> These books contain sketches of his attempt to relay the knowledge. They are sketches of his attempt to

create an artistic dissemination of the understanding about ascension. These books have not been viewed by many and are sought after by the Vatican library.

Why is it important for us to know about Michelangelo's books?

There is an assembly of writings that are derived from the information that was relayed in the Sinaitic experience. These writings and ideas have been conveyed to Michelangelo. The documentation of these ideas contains a similar awareness to what you are working on in this book or volume. The belief that Michelangelo was also made aware of our world is conclusive in the writings.

You mentioned earlier, "There is a new order in place that is waiting to take over the responsibility for these works". What exactly are you referring to?

The reason for the containment of the books and the works including miscellaneous drawings is that there is a need for this information that will be revealed in the upcoming events that occur in 2034. There is a safe keeping of written documents that will be used at a "future time". There are people who are aware of the existence of the writings and the books that are contained. They will be utilized at an important place and space in the evolution and change of the world dynamic.

How can we prove that these books exist?

This will be perceived as a conspiracy mission on your part. There is no exact proof of the existence of these books in your linear time period. Your readers must understand that Michelangelo's contribution extends beyond his artwork. The collective association of artists in this time period is affiliated with our world. These artists made the time travel to fulfill the mission of the Repair Project and disseminate in the form of Earth Beings such as Michelangelo.

Did Michelangelo just walk into town as a stranger one day and make up his own origin story?

The plan for the Being known as Michelangelo was exactly as you are depicting. He made a journey through the Iridis gateway experience and undertook a mission for dissemination. This would rely on a narrative and an explanation.

History tells us that his father was Leonardo Buonarroti and his mother was Francesca Di Neri. He was born in Caprese and lost his mother to illness at 6 years old.

He put into practice the Iridis Gateway. The belief that the Being Michelangelo is originating in a human birth experience is not a correct description. The historical accounts are representational of the alliances and agreements that were made during this historical linear time period.

Many readers will perceive this as a fictional tale.

The idea is not easily absorbable as it does come across as absurd in the description. Beings who are able to experience time travel are also able to completely fit in and undertake the responsibility of dissemination. When you experience time travel you are instantly involved in the experience. There is no preparation such as school or the experience of having to be birthed. The birth symbolism or analogy is the gateway of the Iridis construct and experience. When you make the time travel experience you are in the experience. There is no preparation. You are in the experience.

Michelangelo arrived via the Iridis gateway, just as Jesus did. Is that an accurate understanding?

This is correct. He voluntarily made the connection with the Earth plane in the similar way that other Beings have, including Jesus.

What world is he from?

He is from the world that awaits you beyond the Lyra threshold. The world beyond the Lyra threshold is a world that you are equating with the understanding of the Eden experience and the Lemuria state.

What exactly is this world?

There is little use in discussing what lies beyond Lyra without first absorbing the tools for ascension. We will discuss the worlds beyond Lyra once you have fully absorbed the information of the Light Body reassembly. At this place and space we recommend that you continue your discussion about artists.

What can we know about Michelangelo's contemporary, Leonardo Da Vinci? What was his role during this time period?

There was and is an undertaking to affront the present paradigm. The Being Da Vinci is part of an alliance group whose mission is to awaken the reconnection of those Beings who are effectively contained and imprisoned in the Earth plane existence. Please ask about specific artwork.

What can you tell us about Da Vinci's Vitruvian man?

This is a clear dissemination of the concept of the sphere and time travel. The depiction is fairly evident. The understanding that shapes are used to guide the construct of the artwork is what was mostly absorbed by the masses. The intention was and continues to be the use of the sphere as in the sphere that contains the Light Being, once the reassembly in Lyra is complete.

Why was Da Vinci sketching objects that resembled tanks, canons and helicopters? Was he designing futuristic war machines?

Da Vinci's concern was that a war on a cosmic scale was on the verge of breaking out. The designs were not necessarily designs that he intended to have constructed. They were designs that he bore witness to in a previous incarnation where there was dramatic warfare and conflict.

What exactly did he witness?

He was describing for this time period the "future" event you refer to as World War II.

How did he have a "previous incarnation" in a future reality?

Man Being perceives time as a linear experience. It is best that your readers do not fixate on the concepts of "past" and "future". We are discussing "history" in your linear terms while you absorb new concepts and belief streams. Be aware however that once the time travel modality is achieved, the distinction of "past" and "future" is not applied.

We read about a rivalry between Michelangelo and Da Vinci. Why would they be rivals if they were part of an alliance?

There was a rivalry in that Michelangelo was more impressed upon to share information and Da Vinci was not encouraged to disseminate as freely. The rivalry that you are depicting is more of an instruction or a series of instructions. Michelangelo was not as restricted as Da Vinci was, although the output that you are describing is definitely more controversial in terms of Da Vinci's work.

Yet you're saying Da Vinci was not given full reign to disseminate.

The frustration that Da Vinci was experiencing is that there was a condition not to reveal information whereas Michelangelo did not have these same parameters.

Why was he restricted?

Da Vinci was emphatically trapped in the Earth plane, whereas Michelangelo had and continues to have allowance to make the experience through the Iridis gateway.

When you say that Da Vinci was "trapped" are you suggesting that he chose not to disconnect? Did he choose the reincarnation cycle?

This is a correct understanding. Da Vinci became trapped and is trapped in his own construct of thinking about experience as a paradigm of manifesting a beginning and an end. The construct that he was responsible for disseminating was not available to him.

There is another Florentine artist, Dante Alighieri, who seemed to have some very specific ideas. What was he trying to convey through his "Divine Comedy"?

NOTE: Dante Alighieri was an Italian poet, born c. 1265 AD in Florence. His epic poem "The Divine Comedy", which describes his journey through Hell, Purgatory and Heaven is widely considered one of the greatest literary works of the Middle Ages. The work is also famous for its exaltation of a woman named Beatrice – for whom Dante declared his love.

The message that is contained in the work is the effectiveness of the regime of religious institution. The loosely contained parables in the work and the divine intervention is somewhat lost on the audience. The reason for the creation of this work is his frustration that the general population is too blind to see.

81

On the surface, Dante's Divine Comedy feels like a religious treatise on morality and faith.

> There are instructions in the paradigms on ascension and the paradigms pertaining to political conquest and religious affirmation. The amusing situation is often frustrated by the fact that nobody understood the real message in the work.

What does Beatrice represent in Dante's work?

> Beatrice represents someone and something that you may all attain. All of you are Beatrice. Beatrice is the belief in ascension and the belief in the world of reassembly and re-acquaintance with the soul ascension group. She represents the belief in the dynamic that you are equipped to reorganize and reconnect with those experiences and the light that belongs to you.

Is that why Dante professes his undying love and admiration for her?

> The archetype of Beatrice and the profound description of the love that he has for her, resemble the assembly of truths. Beatrice represents the truth and Dante's revelation that she is a Being in its full capacity. This inspires him to equate that with love. Beatrice is representing a guidance and mission to disseminate the understanding that there is more choice in the existence that awaits those who make a disconnect.

There is speculation that the real life Beatrice Portinari is Dante's Beatrice. Is this true?

> This is incorrect. Correlating Beatrice with a human that existed in the world of Dante is not a truthful explanation. Beatrice is an archetype in Dante's written works. This archetype was inspired by Dante's communication with a Light Being.

Dante was communicating with a Light Being, which he then represented through the character of Beatrice. Is that a correct understanding?

> This is correct. Beatrice can be regarded as a Being who communicated with the artist. This Being assisted him in collecting and absorbing the understanding of the primordial existence and the worlds beyond.

What passage do you recommend we explore in Dante's Divine Comedy?

> First examine Canto XXXII, in the book referred to as "Purgatory". There is a truthful account of the way that Dante operates and collects and absorbs information. This represents a similar approach in your own undertaking.

NOTE: The cited passage is within Canto XXXII of Purgatory.

"Therefore, for that world's good which liveth ill,
Fix on the car thine eyes, and what thou seest,
Having returned to Earth, take heed though write"

In this Canto, Dante also describes the assembly of a Giant, a Whore and Horned Beasts. What is being represented?

> Beatrice offers a prophecy pertaining to this assembly in the following chapter. Please refer your readers to this passage.

NOTE: The cited passage is within Canto XXXIII of Purgatory.

"Within which a Five-hundred, Ten and Five,
One sent from God, shall slay the thievish woman,
And that same Giant who is sitting with her"

Can you explain what the "Whore" represents?

> The depiction of the "whore" as you are referring to represents the hoarding of knowledge and the hoarding of the gateway. The word "whore" or "prostitute" is not an accurate explanation and the word has been misconstrued and changed over your linear time span. We believe that the continued fulfillment of the blocked gateway is now being corrected in your dissemination.

What is Dante's specific guidance in this passage?

> The guidance here is to stop believing in the blocked gateway. The reference to the female and the beasts in the passage is an explanation that there is no fear to encounter our world, as the experience is seamless and uneventful. Entering our world is not a massive undertaking and experience. The idea that courage is needed to encounter our world is also an incorrect and unfortunate belief.

What does the assembly of the Giant, the Whore and the Beasts represent?

> The Beings depicted in the passage and accompanied artwork are representational of the fears and the fear mongering that continues. They represent the hijacking and hoarding of ascension knowledge.

Please explain the prophecy of "Five Hundred, Ten and Five" that is referenced in that passage.

> The understanding of the cryptic message refers to a passage in your linear historical context. The "Five Hundred" is the 500 years that have elapsed since the beginning of the corruption of the church and the obstruction of the gateway experience. This began 500 years before Dante's dissemination of the Divine Comedy.

What does "Ten" refer to?

> The "Ten" is designating how many changes in the belief structure will occur. There are 10 desecrations and fragmentations and re-assemblies of belief. There are 10 primary organizations that will discontinue in the 5th event. These events parallel what occurred 500 years before the dissemination of Dante's Divine Comedy. The similar pattern of experience will repeat.

NOTE: Dante's Divine Comedy was completed in 1320 AD. Five centuries prior, Constantinople (modern day Istanbul) was the capital of the Eastern Roman Empire known as the Byzantine Empire. The "parallel events" being referenced are the conflicts between the growing Islamic Empire and Byzantine.

Please explain what you mean by "fragmentation of beliefs".

There was and will be a designation and change in geographic boundaries that will result in a huge political upheaval. This will equate with a situation that causes religious instability and a derailment in a financial sector that pertains to resources. The belief that war is necessary is a natural outcome of these experiences. The birth of a new nation led by a Being who is controversial and continues a lineage and a dynasty that is not beneficial to the West. We are describing the expansion and change in what you are defining as the "Middle East" in your current linear historical timeline.

What does the "Five" represent in Beatrice's prophecy?

There have been five Beings, each representing a cycle and gateway experience. These five Beings and cycles have been opportunities for Beings to take the homeward journey of ascension. We are approaching the fifth cycle or experience. This is equivalent to a Messiah experience. There have been numerous Beings who have assisted in Man Being's ascension but there have been five critical Beings, the last of which will arrive in the linear time of 2034.

Who are the five Messiah figures?

The five Messiahs are operating in a group. They are from the same soul ascension group experience and they include Abraham, Akhenaten, Moses, Jesus and the final Messiah figure in 2034. We will continue this discussion in a further dissemination, as your readers will desire ample preparation for this event.

Is Purgatory Dante's representation of the intermediary world of Lyra?

> Dante's work was an attempt to disseminate this information, yes. The idea that there is a purification is a belief that there is another world. This world contains your own world of belief and experience with your ascension group. The completion of the soul group experience and assembly of the Light Being and the Light Being containment is an important concept to master and absorb. We are calling it a concept, as there is no understanding until there is an experience and coinciding belief.

Another prolific and celebrated writer comes to mind – William Shakespeare. Thirteen of his plays are set in Italy and several of his plots contain Italian elements. Was he also part of this allegiance?

> Shakespeare was given information and instructed on the tools of ascension. He wanted to continue to seek out more learning and instruction and encourage the masses to be aware that this ascension experience was occurring in the geographical area of Italy.

Are ascension events always designated a specific geographic location?

It is not a situation that is dependent upon a geographical construct. The situation was such that the Beings made their way to this place in the Earth plane and congregated there for the ascension dissemination experience. The prolific artistry that you are referring to in Florence during the time period of the Medici Family is also an example of the idea that the construct of a universal shift in awareness is an effort en masse and is a calculated undertaking.

Does an artistic movement usually accompany an ascension event?

There will be artistry in a prolific and unbounded experience that begins in the late 2020s in your historical linear accounts. This artistic expression will be on par with what has occurred in this linear time period that you are describing as the Medici dynasty.

Being "on par" with the Medici artists suggests that there are virtuoso artists coming our way.

There are Beings who are present in the Earth plane density who are awaiting the instructions and the instruction will be to disseminate en masse. The ascension experience requires everyone to participate. It is initialized and instigated by a group of Beings who are making the initial steps of the gateway reconnection to be known.

Is this book the initial instruction?

This book and its subsequent volumes, along with the accompanying discoveries will serve as the forerunner to the upcoming ascension experience. Instruction has been given throughout your linear history, as was the case with the Being you refer to as Shakespeare.

What more can you tell us about Shakespeare?

This Being believed that there was more to human existence. His interest was thinly veiled in some of his stories and accounts. There was assistance. These stories or ideas for stories were not communicated to him directly but to a woman that he was involved with.

Who was the woman and what was their involvement?

The stories were communicated to his sister Joan.

How were they communicated to her?

She was modified with the ability to communicate directly with our world.

So Joan was connecting with Light Beings and Shakespeare weaved this information into his plays and stories?

This is correct. His information was not of his own divine connection. What he chose to do with the information is undoubtedly his pen but the source is not his own. He obtained the information and played with the meaning.

Are there more modern artists we can discuss that were/are consciously disseminating ascension ideas?

> Please explore the artist known as Van Gogh. There is inherent symbolism and quality to his art that illustrates the connection that Van Gogh had with Light Being contact, including the profound way he used paint color and light. His awareness that we are all Light Beings was and is exceptional. If we can all see each other in the fashion that he chooses to paint we will be able to ascend more readily. Look at the light and the way that it is communicated.

What can you tell us about the so-called "27 Club"? Why have talented artists been dying at this specific age? Is there a reason other than drug and alcohol abuse?

NOTE: The "27 Club" refers to a group of artists that have all died tragically at the age of 27. Some of the more recent and famous individuals include Jim Morrison (The Doors), Janis Joplin, Jimi Hendrix, Brian Jones (The Rolling Stones), Kurt Cobain (Nirvana), Amy Winehouse, Jean Michel Basquiat (graffiti artist/painter), Anton Yelchin (actor).

> The 27 Club is an organization of beliefs and composed of many individual Light Beings who are contained in an assembly of one Being of experience. The Beings are all in a unified alliance. The 27 Club specifically involves Beings who are making a travel in time to disseminate and share artistically in the Earth dimension.

You're saying that they are "many individual Beings contained in an assembly of one Being of experience". Is this how a soul ascension group operates?

This is one way in which a soul ascension group can assemble. This group however is not the same species of Beings that you are defined as.

What species are they?

This is a cooperation with an assembly that is aligned with the Pleiades experience. This may seem somewhat strange or questionable to your readers but these Beings are experiencing a human form in order to disseminate through the arts.

NOTE: Pleiades is a well-known and documented star cluster. It is one of the closest star clusters to Earth. Several of its brightest stars can be viewed with the naked eye.

The notion that another species incarnates among us – or even exists – will sound absurd to a lot of people.

What Man Being defines as "absurd" often serves as an indicator of what requires further examination. Man Being ridicules what he does not wish to assimilate and experience. "Absurdity" does not equate to non-existent.

Back to the 27 Club, why do they overdose or drive themselves to an early death?

They are behaving and contributing to an early demise that will occur regardless. It is similar to the way that you all are coping with your existence in the imprisoned Earth density experience. For these Beings the intensity of their own experiences are triggering a need to experience in all levels, including drugs and alcohol and other questionable activities. This is a consequence and a clashing of the need to experience unrestricted dissemination in such a short period.

Is the main obstacle for artists that Earth is a restrictive plane of existence?

The Artist does not perceive boundaries. The problem that exists is that unrestricted dissemination is not welcomed or allowed and there is a clash that is very unique that is occurring. The early demise at 27 represents the limitations of the experience that will continue again and again with other Beings who choose to disseminate and are arriving here as part of the collective mission.

Why 27 and not 28 or 26?

The energetic experience of these Beings is not similar to your experience. The "27" represents a unique experience in that the energy assembly has reached the limitation of containment. These Beings are not able to exist in a physical contained form much as you are experiencing in the Earth plane density. There is a limitation much like you not being able to breathe under water for an extended period of time. This is the physics of the Light Body containment.

The 27-year timeframe is the natural lifespan of a Light Body on Earth and not a planned event. Is that an accurate understanding?

This is correct. It does have a unique lifespan and ability. The linear 27 years represents the limitations of containment. This does not resemble a planned execution of a preexisting blueprint. This is the limitation of the light. The light cannot be contained for an extended period of time. This is a unique experience whereby these Beings cannot be contained beyond this amount of linear time.

Will these Beings continue to perform this mission?

This will continue to occur and when you see other Beings existing at this time in your linear accounts you will understand that they are also uniquely involved in this experience. It represents a type of species and a type of existence. This is energy that can be contained for a limited amount of your linear time experience.

Can you give us an example of a living artist who is committed to the Repair Project and disseminating information?

There is an artist who operates on a level of anonymity. This is an artist who is known globally. We would like to point out to you that the individual you believe is secretly installing artwork in public spaces worldwide is affiliated with a group of Beings that are currently working in your planet to change some of the incorrect ideas that you have absorbed. This individual is not working alone as has been suggested. We will refer to this artist as "Artist X".

Is Artist X creating the artwork on his/her own or with a group?

There is a group of individuals involved in disseminating the information or creating the artwork. Artist X is an example of an individual that is making an impact and a change in the shifting of the conscious beliefs. What is also occurring however, is the interruption and the intervention of marketing and commercializing and the degenerating of the initial intention.

Is Artist X's work really having an impact on the collective consciousness?

The artwork does not appear to be as serious as it intends. This is the way that this group is choosing to disseminate and behave with respect to sharing codes and transmitting ideas. There does not have to be a serious perception or attitude toward disseminating information. Entertainment can be a vehicle for dissemination. The intention of this Group is quite a serious one but the understanding from "authorities" is that this is not anything that needs to be worrisome or taken seriously.

Will Artist X's identity ever be revealed?

There will be a definite event that involves a new understanding of who this Artist is. There will be a sighting and the Artist X team will be implicated.

What exactly will occur?

There will be a visual interpretation of an event to come and when it is noticed that this event was depicted and foretold in the artwork there will be an understanding that this Artist has the knowledge of the existence of Light Beings. The event is a sighting.

A sighting of what?

There will be a definite sighting of what many of you refer to as "UFOs". This definition will be discussed in further dialogue. The sighting will take place in Brisbane, Australia.

Who are the Light Beings that Artist X is in communication with?

This group is connected with a Star System that is not part of your Galaxy. The amusing anecdote here is that it is right under all of your noses. There are many ongoing experiences like this that some of you may not pay serious attention to, as you feel that it is "light" or "trite" or not of any consequence. There are many that are operating in this style and character as they feel it is offering more impact by the subtly of the dissemination. The messages are in fact very clear but the dissemination style may not be.

It appears that artists wield more influence than we've given them credit for.

Artists have a responsibility to disseminate awareness and the codes for awareness. The Artist brings proof and evidence of those things that lie beyond your existence and beyond your awareness of this existence. We encourage your readership to assimilate this belief.

9

Concealments

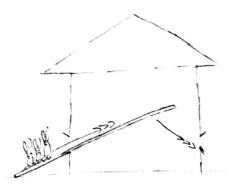

The Artist X project is a benevolent operation but there are other organizations and perceived concealments that we'd like to address. Would it be useful to address some "conspiracy theories"?

> Man Being uses the term "conspiracy" as a weapon to silence those Beings who seek the truth. This is not an insight. It is an unfortunate reality.

Is there currently a cure for cancer that is being withheld from us?

> It is hardly a revelation for your readers that there is in fact exceptional research and understanding that is not being utilized. The companies and the Beings who control the information are not allowing this to be disseminated to the public for the reason of financial gain and benefit. The more appropriate question is: How can Man Being prevent cancer?

How can Man Being prevent cancer?

> The relationship between cancer and the frequencies from the cellular phone network is also a "conspiracy theory". Cancer is being created as a way to control and contain communication through the cellular phone network exchange.

Are you saying that cell phones have been deliberately created to cause cancer and prevent our ascension?

> This is a correct understanding. There is a relationship between the way Man Being must communicate now and the relationship of the perpetual cancer making agenda. Cancer and

97

communication are unfortunately aligned. The cellular phone network is creating cancer by creating communication and frequencies that your cells should not be absorbing.

Readers will still want to know what the magic medicine is. You speak of prevention but what is the cure that is being withheld?

It is the prevention of cancer that is the understanding that you must subscribe to. The understanding that there are medicines to heal cancer is not the answer.

Is doing away with our cell phone the only prevention strategy?

Plant communication in terms of the plant cell network is also what is needed. The understanding that Nature heals is correct. The instabilities in the Earth plane that are destroying your identity with a natural existence are contributing to the inability to heal. The conspiracy that medicine and healing is being withheld is somewhat accurate but what is being withheld is the prevention of the cancer. By destroying trees and vegetation and perpetuating the diet and the consumption that requires the destruction of trees and plants, you are perpetuating a situation where there is no prevention of cancer available.

Having a plant diet and existing within a natural environment is the best prevention. Is that what you're saying?

It is the simplicity of this truth that confounds Man Being. Cancer is an extreme situation whereby there is no longer communication with trees and plants. The balance of what we are calling "Nature" is in place to protect us. This is why Man Being is often driven to spend time "in the woods" as a means to "recharge".

We'd also like to discuss whether we should we be vaccinating our children. Some government agencies require parents to immunize their children for things like the measles, rubella, tetanus, polio, diphtheria etc.

Vaccination is a way to stunt the cells so that we can no longer absorb new ideas and new awareness. The idea that we are protecting the cells is limiting the knowledge and absorption.

What is the right action to take when our child is faced with the threat of any of these diseases?

Cancer is the bigger problem than these diseases. Until you remove the mechanisms that are creating damage on the cells and until you remove those instruments that are allowing you to absorb destructive communication that is ultimately creating cancer, there is no way to prevent the other diseases.

We understand that this goes beyond vaccinations but schools are requiring immunization and some parents are vehemently opposed.

Unless you are able to provide an environment whereby your children can absorb a plant based diet and the energy and healing and information from nature, there is no recommendation to necessarily stop the vaccination. The frustration for many parents is that the healing and energy from the plant is not necessarily available to those Beings who live in the urban environment and developed world.

This is a no-win situation.

This is an exceptionally problematic undertaking in that the intention to remove the disease causing agents is somewhat futile. The element of protection that a vaccination may provide is inconsequential with respect to the agents of cancer causing disease. However, the discomfort and instability that is created by removing the opportunity to vaccinate for now outweighs the difficulty that is created if your children are not vaccinated. It is an unfortunate conundrum. There is no solution with the current ways of Man Being. Dietary and the socio-economic and industrial norms are all promoting cancer and cancer causing communication.

Is there anything more nefarious going on with the vaccination program? Are we being injected with further diseases that Pharmaceutical companies are capitalizing on?

This may have been a platform or idea but the cell phone and cellular network is now taking over. Your reliance on the cellular phone network is the grand "conspiracy" you are inquiring about. What is curious is that the majority of Beings in the Earth plane are aware of this but remain committed to their own demise.

Our reliance on cell phone technology is also tied in with our use of the Internet and Social Media. What can you tell us about these Social Media platforms and the Big Tech Companies that produce cell phone technology?

The only reason to create these organizations and parameters is to control the census. This is in lieu of a census taking.

Are these companies simply in place to track human beings and monitor their activity?

This is their only contribution.

Moving on to conspiracies pertaining to political and historical events, we'd like to ask about President John F Kennedy. Why was he assassinated in 1963 and why is there a continued cover up of the assassination details?

Your questions about vaccination, cancer and cellular phones overlap with your question about this President. The Being known as JFK was aware of the undertaking that was being developed in Russia to create a program and a condition for monitoring the public. He did not agree with the monitoring of people on a massive scale. There was an agreement that he was being asked to participate in. It was an agreement between countries that there would be monitoring. He did not want to subscribe to this secret agreement.

What specifically can you tell us about this secret agreement?

101

JFK was going to speak out against a certain cultural evolution or norm that would be promoted through the agreement of the United Nations. There was a global initiative to control the masses and also control their own expiry dates. The lifespan of the masses was to be controlled and instrumental to the alliance between the countries. This is not something that JFK was willing to participate in.

This is extraordinarily vile.

What is more alarming is that JFK's alliances were few and far between as he took a stance against this position.

Does this scheme to "control our expiry dates" tie in with our reliance on cell phones?

This is correct. There are many ways to monitor and control the lifespan and the built-in death experience by introducing agents and elements of disease. The objective would be an agreed upon expiry date of Beings who are located in different countries. There was an agreement that the population control through these agents of disease would be implemented. JFK was not willing to participate or sign the agreement.

Which country or countries proposed this?

Russia and the USA. There was a globally agreed upon agenda to eradicate people through a control of their lifespan by introducing the disease and cancer causing agents such as the cellular phone network.

102

This is disgusting. Companies have ensured that the cell phone is our lifeblood.

Yes.

What else is being done to control the population?

The monitoring of water and the bodies of water that exist in your Earth plane are damaged. The problem and the interchangeable notion that correction of water quality is through the introduction of chemicals is a moot strategy. The reason is the dynamics and the interplay of your cellular constitution does not allow for the required change in the chemistry of the water, specifically drinking water.

Many people believe that our water is intentionally contaminated.

The molecules of the water must be of a certain shape and size to allow for an effective registration in your cellular makeup. There is a change in your cellular makeup because of the irresponsible management of the water quality and the introduction of isotopes into the drinking water worldwide, as legislation is allowing this to occur.

There isn't enough public outrage on this issue.

There is a lack of awareness of what structures are being introduced into your tap water specifically. You are being made to consume unusual components in the drinking water, which contain minerals that are somewhat radioactive in nature.

103

This is occurring to continue the program to disrupt Man Being's ascension.

Contaminating our water is the ultimate weapon, isn't it?

There is a measure from space that can determine the isotope that is being released into the atmosphere. The consequence of this experience is that you are unwittingly being involved in military operations unbeknownst to you all. The cellular signal and communication can be used in this way as well and will continue. You are an army whether or not you are subscribing to participate. You are unwittingly and unknowingly participating in these experiments.

We can throw away our cell phones but we can't stop drinking water. Is there any way to repair the water we drink?

If the water is exposed to a frequency between 600-750 Hz, this can eliminate and break down the foreign molecules to effectively heal the water. This requires a device that will play or create this sound. The exposure time must be approximately 12 hours and 6 minutes.

If we don't take action to correct this what is the impact on our physical health?

Most importantly, you are not able to make the proper ascension absorption and journey if your balance and instability is off. The infiltration of the foreign molecules in your drinking water creates a disturbance cognitively. This is an alarming situation that will reach an epidemic level in fifteen linear years. The physical damage is affecting the inner ear specifically and the processing in your brain that allows for balance. There is an alarming increase in the number of Beings that are experiencing instability in their physical movements.

Are there any other nefarious programs like this that we're unaware of?

There is a disturbance so that when you are walking on the ground there is vibration that is being created from the explosive activity that is undertaken by various government and military projects. The vibration is being absorbed in your physical form and is creating an electrical channel that is disturbing your heart functioning. The activities are occurring worldwide in different schedules.

How exactly is this "disturbing our heart functioning"?

There is an unprecedented amount of Beings on the planet that are experiencing heart trouble and heart attacks. The general attributes such as "poor eating" and "lifestyle" will be the factors to blame. You are unaware that there is a correlation between your heart condition and the military operations we are describing.

What exactly is the nature of this military operation?

They are testing new weaponry that is being promoted worldwide and attempting to be the first to accomplish the successful creation of these weapons of mass destruction.

105

What do you mean by "worldwide"? Are there several countries conducting these experiments?

> The USA has a testing facility in Peru and Paraguay, for example. They have alliances everywhere that are not actually in alliance with them but agreements are in place. There is a program that will ultimately join with the USA and help to create a monumental weapon. This weapon will be used to threaten other countries in 2027, linear time.

In the meantime, it's being used on the general public.

> The disruption of the heart activity is creating an epidemic in heart health. These weapons of mass destruction are killing Beings before a war even begins.

Is there a way to protect our hearts from this?

> There will be the creation and invention of socks and garments with copper threading that someone is developing.

Is there a reason heart disease is higher with men than with women?

> Males are able to absorb more charge as well as able to absorb more energy in the left ventricle of the heart, as the construction of the physical heart in a male species is of a slightly different shape and quality.

What is the name of this military operation?

P.U.T.A.W.

What does that stand for?

"Project Terror Assembly Weaponry". The "U" is a code comprised of the letters "UWRI". It is a code within a code.

On the topic of government and military operations, what is being conducted at Area 51?

There is a clean up project. Area 51 is being repurposed. The important thing to note of Area 51 is a strategic energy transmission focused specifically at Mexico and the whole Southern part of the USA. This transmission is occurring to block or prevent a gateway from being accessed. There is a shift in an energy gradient that is not beneficial for our purpose.

Is the US Military trying to obstruct humans from Light Travel?

Yes.

Are there ETs working at area 51?

There have been visitations by Beings from Andromeda. This is not beneficial.

Are ETs responsible for the Nazca Lines? What is their function?

The Nazca Lines are aligned with the Sirius agenda. The purpose of these lines is to modulate visitation.

107

Originally the lines were installed specifically for a visitation of Sirius Beings. What the lines indicate are how something enters into an atmosphere or a density/dimension – how it moves from one density to another and how it must align itself into an energy grid. Energy grids must be aligned with this so you know how to move in and out of the Earth gradient.

We'd like to shift to historical ruins and artifacts. Who built the Stonehenge and what is it for?

The Stonehenge is not necessarily accurately described. The stones or stone fragments are stolen and modified from another structure.

What was the other structure?

The pieces in the Stonehenge are borrowed from another structure that was in the original shape of a tetrahedron or pyramid. This structure is not original or complete.

Wouldn't that be obvious to archeologists or scholars or architects who've studied the Stonehenge?

Man Being wants to believe that this structure is the original because it serves a purpose to benefit the narrative of their own personal culture and system that they are adhering to. Many have secretly asked themselves "why am I adhering to this narrative that is inconclusive". The pieces in this structure are borrowed from another important structure that no longer exists. There was a pyramid shape that existed nearby.

Why was the Pyramid taken apart?

> The Pyramid was destroyed as a marker or a celebration that would indicate a gateway was obstructed and would no longer be accessed. It is a cover up in denying the origins. It is a cover up in denying that we once were present.

What year was it destroyed?

> The Pyramid was destroyed in 6500 BC. The pieces were sitting there and over time they were borrowed.

How was the Stonehenge built? Did humans have the engineering to construct it?

> Not humans. Andromeda Beings.

What was their purpose in constructing this?

> They believed they would set up a homestead there, which was not permitted.

What was the Antikythera and who invented it?

NOTE: The Antikythera is an artifact that was retrieved in 1901 off the coast of the Greek Island Kythera. The belief is that it was used to predict celestial phenomena and astronomical positions, years in advance.

> This application was borrowed. The first application was originally practiced in Egypt.

It's being called an ancient Greek analogue computer.

The origin of this version of the device is Greek. The device was originally brought to Africa and was involved in helping Man Being build and think about resonance in their structures. The purpose that the Greeks developed is a modified application, closer to a clock. The clock measured travel and time in terms of our stars and what you call planetary and cosmic presences. What this was originally intended for was a precise measurement to create sacred geometry design to allow further understanding of resonance in form. We will discuss the tetrahedron or pyramid shape. This device was brought to allow further building in this context so Man Being would align himself in correct formation, cellular and bio-magnetic. The current application is a modified clock.

What can you tell us about Qin Shi Huang's Terracotta Army?

NOTE: In 1974 a local farmer in Shaanxi, China came across what would eventually be the discovery of almost 8000 Terracotta Warriors – commissioned by China's first Emperor Qin Shi Huang. Each statue has a unique face and they were originally arranged in military formation. Some scholars have called it the Archeological Discovery of the 20th century.

The Emperor had knowledge about the Light Body assembly much like you have. This is how he left his mark.

What do the statues represent?

The statues represent the army of enlightened Souls who are assembling and making the ascension journey. There is an undertaking to disseminate belief about ascension in this part of the world. The understanding that there have been Beings and events such as a Messiah event in different parts of the world is now being slowly revealed. When we are describing a Messiah event we are describing it in terms of an event of this stature but not necessarily pointing to a Messiah Being.

Do the number of statues found correlate with the exact number of ascended Beings?

The number of statues that remain are an exacting truth in that there have been this many souls that have documented the ascension experience. There have been this many Beings that have attempted to disseminate awareness much like what you are undertaking in this book.

Are these statues representing all Beings that have ever ascended?

There have been this many attempts to release information and there have been this many Beings who have written documentation and have made an ascension event. The creation of these Beings and the remembrance of these events is what is being displayed in the concentration and calculated dissemination of the discovery of these Beings. The discovery of the Beings is also part of a Repair Project and dissemination. Again, the discovery of the statues is part of an undertaking much like what you are involved in with your own Repair Project.

Is it accurate to say that Qin Shi Huang was another Akhenaten figure?

> This is accurate. The principles that are adhered to are identical to the principles that Akhenaten adhered to. This is an identical experience.

Was Emperor Qin Shi Huang also subscribing to the Aten principle that Akhenaten introduced?

> The Emperor aligned by the star and in the discovery of the pit and the Terracotta Warrior assembly there are other pieces of information and physical artifacts that were removed from the pit. The description about the alignment with the star had been removed. There is not a complete installation of relics that is available to the public, as what is being shown there is what you are allowed to see. His beliefs are not something that is available for public use or public consumption.

What was the specific description about the alignment with the star that is being concealed?

> There is an object that has a similar shape and design as the Aten. It is in the shape of a human eye. There are extensions from the eye similar to the design and presentation of the Aten and its outstretched arms.

Can you explain once again what this symbol represents?

> The understanding of this description is an escape from the Judgment experience that we have already described in our discussions pertaining to the

biblical accounts. The Chinese Emperor chose to escape from the reality of the reincarnation stream of existence. The scholars that he was aligned with initially did not subscribe to this information and did not wish this information to be released as this would result in an instability of the union of the geographic regions that were being reassembled under the Emperor's control.

Much has been written about Emperor Qin Shi Huang's military conquests and also his killing of some 460 Confucian followers. History does not describe him as an enlightened man.

This is a very confusing dilemma as he started his reign in one state of awareness and shifted into another state of awareness. This is what gave the impression of his instability, mentally and emotionally. The detail of his being completely out of control and obsessed with power derives from the sudden shift in his beliefs. In the 32nd year of his linear life as the written accounts are suggesting, there was a seminal and pivotal shift in his beliefs that he encountered through his pursuit of alchemical knowledge. Much of the information that he retained was disseminated through his dreams and allowed for his new understanding and new obligations in the Repair Project.

Did he actually kill the Confucian scholars?

These "scholars" were not aligned with the reassembly experience of the Light Body and the understanding that their ideas were killed off or

113

equated with a suppression is a correct understanding.

Is the historical account inaccurate? Was he killing off ideas or people?

> There were attempts on the Emperor's life and only those individuals received a death penalty. These deaths were designed to contain those scholars who were attempting to murder the Emperor. He was disseminating a correct awareness about the ability to ascend. This understanding and belief was in opposition to the assembly of scholars that were involved in the control of the masses by correct rules of behaviour and social conduct.

Is the current Chinese government aware of these truths about Emperor Qin Shi Huang?

> They have recently adjusted their thinking and decision about what experience this Being had. There is also information about this Emperor held in the Vatican Archive of written material and accounts. The Chinese government is more closely aligned with the responsibility to hoard information in the Vatican archives than you are aware of. There is an alignment with all the political and governing factions with this repository of knowledge, including the mysterious alignment with the USA.

A discussion about the Vatican Library is long overdue.

> Please be aware that there is a united assembly to suppress information about the ascension experiences that are shared in the historical, biblical

and spiritual accounts worldwide. The reason that this information has not been completely suppressed or maintained is that there are oral histories and transmissions that you cannot contain.

What knowledge is the Vatican most intent on concealing?

They believe that an awareness of other worlds will not serve their purpose. This is an obvious truth and invaluable and there has been a serious problem of misinformation since 1634 AD. This year in your historical timeline is important in that the considerations in the ideology and cosmologies of this time were rearranged so that you would no longer be able to see the truth.

What exactly are you referring to?

There was a trial that involved the Being known as Galileo. This event was a significant setback for Man Being's understanding of cosmology.

NOTE: This was the year that Galileo's "Dialogo" was placed on the index of forbidden books by the Vatican. In it he supported a heliocentric view of the solar system. He was later made to deny his beliefs under the threat of death.

The Vatican discussion could be its own book.

The Vatican in principle should be an easy discussion but the ramifications are far reaching.

What else is the Vatican Library safeguarding?

In the Vatican assembly there is a Treaty. The document of which has not seen the light of day in many centuries. There was a choice to remain on your planet that was instigated in 920 BC following the reign of King Solomon. The content of this Treaty explains how Man Being is not in complete awareness or agreement with his Earth plane existence.

NOTE: Solomon was the son and heir to King David – of the United Kingdom of Israel. The conventional dates of his reign are ca. 970-930 BC. According to the Hebrew Bible Solomon built the First Temple or Holy Temple in ancient Jerusalem. Upon Solomon's death, the ten Northern tribes began to rebel and the Kingdom was divided once again.

Was the choice to leave the Earth plane an ascension event?

Yes, we are of speaking about the ascension opportunity. The ruling Empire during this time period created an alliance with the visiting Orion DRA. The treaty and the document that is inscribed in stone and stone pieces is housed in the Vatican. It details the intention of Orion DRA to rule and control the resources on your planet.

Did King Solomon design the Treaty?

This is incorrect. The assembly beneath King Solomon was responsible. King Solomon did not contemplate or create the treaty. The political advisors who were adversarial were conspiring to create a new world order by this treaty. There was in your linear accounts a conspiracy to topple his jurisdiction and power and the accounts in the written disseminations are more or less correct.

To clarify, this group of conspirators signed Earth's resources over to Orion DRA in exchange for temporal power. Is this an accurate understanding?

> This treaty is a decision that will allow the mining of resources and the free allowance for this activity should it be needed in the future. The resources are also including Man Being, as there is a need to utilize Beings in a program of proliferation. The enslavement and the agenda to occupy the Earth plane as it continues today is a remnant of this treaty and experience.

Instead of helping Mankind to achieve "spiritual salvation", the Vatican continues to be complicit in our enslavement.

> This book and the Repair Project undertaking is providing the appropriate amount of outrage and ascension information so that Man Being will once again have the opportunity to return home.

We're going to assume that any discussion about the "Illuminati" would be as revolting.

> The Illuminati and what they stand for today in your human time frame is not what the original idea was. The Illuminati histories and the understanding about the Illuminati span many centuries and many regroupings and reorganization. It is not possible for you to concisely describe this situation in a way that won't be a book unto itself. We can return to this discussion in a subsequent volume.

10

Aeserius and the Pyramids

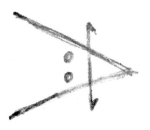

You mentioned the "tetrahedron" in the previous discussion. What is the importance of this shape?

> This shape or design is an effective direction in communication. You are asking about a highly technical way of moving sound around. This shape is also referred to as "Sirius Complex 18.4.3".

Does this concern genetics and DNA?

> Yes. There are properties that we can speak about and will apply to your questions. Your question is a big one.

Which civilizations, if any, have applied this knowledge of the design?

> The Dogon people of Mali, Africa are an example. They have an understanding. They have applied this understanding.

Do they still understand it?

> The understanding has been somewhat what you call "lost" and what we would say is modified. The understanding is no longer the original application.

Please summarize in simpler terms exactly what this shape is/does.

> This shape is how we move. This shape is how we absorb information. This shape is also how we transmit and repair. This particular design allows us to transport between what you refer to as "dimension" or "density". The design collects

119

resonance and also disseminates what you call knowledge and awareness. We advise you to meditate on this shape.

Is this shape essentially how we communicate and move?

Yes. Your cells are composed this way.

Are scientists aware of this design and composition?

They think they are. They believe they have achieved something similar.

Have they?

They are using this in other applications. These applications will not necessarily be of benefit. This is an instance where you have something in your hands but you don't see it. This discussion could have ramifications that improve Mankind. It can also allow some to empower themselves incorrectly and this perhaps is alarming for some.

The Pyramid is a tetrahedron.

Yes.

How was pyramid construction achieved and who built them?

Recall that the tetrahedron facilitates communication and movement. The sand was moved. This sonic achievement you will realize soon. Blocks of physical matter are not described correctly. The sands were moved.

120

We perceive the Pyramids as monuments and as an archeological feat, although there remains a myriad of questions about who achieved the construction and how.

> When you see it in form it does not mean that this is the function. Please remember that Mankind sees in form. We understand and this is what we will correct. Your improvement will be that you no longer need the Pyramids to exist in order for you to accept change. Mankind needs the physical in order to achieve understanding. The awareness is there but you do not see it yet. The Pyramids exist in your mind but we will achieve a new understanding soon. Physical achievements will soon be light achievements. Light does not need the physical expression that you are presently built to experience. Form is not the explanation. It is a way for you to see until you understand how to see.

Are you saying that the Pyramid is a representation of our ability to exist and work with light?

> This is a simplified understanding, yes.

You call the tetrahedron a "Sirius Complex". Is there a connection between the star Sirius and the Pyramids?

> This is an important question and one that requires a shift in your belief patterns. This point will be regarded as a starting point where you will continue to absorb this instruction at a rate that is beneficial for the continued transmission. What needs to be accepted and absorbed is that you will no longer benefit from discussion and absorption of ideas that exist in your Earth density.

121

Does this relate to how our awareness resonates within the tetrahedron shape and within our cellular design?

> This is accurate. The thinking process that you have previously established will not coincide with our messages or our continued transmission with you. If you do not follow our instructions and absorb the information you will not continue to modify. Our instructions will fall out of sync. You will not penetrate to the level required to continue to absorb our communication.

Will our DNA structure remain the same if our belief system doesn't change?

> Yes. There is a corruption in your DNA sequencing, as you have been made aware. This corruption will not allow the messages we provide to you to be absorbed if you continue to reinvent yourselves using your Earth density paradigm. Please shift accordingly.

Please continue with the Sirius information.

> We would like to present to you the name "Aeserius" or what you refer to as "Sirius". This is the Star name that is known to your scientists as the brightest Star in your night sky. What we are presenting to you today is the history of Sirius. It is essential to your continued modification that you absorb this correct and historical account of how Sirius became involved in your current version of your civilization. We are using the word "history" for the purpose of this dialogue and discussion but please remember that this word will no longer bear

any resemblance or any importance once you have mastered the concepts of the time travel paradigm and condition.

The Dogon tribe from Mali you mentioned claim to have been visited by a race of Beings from the Sirius Star System. They called them the "Nommos". The Ancients also recognized the Sirius Star in ritual and religion.

NOTE: In the 1930s, French anthropologists Marcel Griaule and Germain Dieterlen spent fifteen years with the Dogon Tribe and their Elders. It was through this research that they discovered the Dogon traditions and their knowledge of the Sirius Star System.

There has been a misunderstanding and a miscommunication that we would like to correct now. Sirius is not an individual and progressed civilization as some of you have decided. What has transpired is a communication and an instruction that was taken and realigned for a purpose that did not fulfill instructions or requirements. There was a mission and an undertaking to go ahead and repopulate an area on your planet. This undertaking was to prepare for further correction of a re-modified gateway reinstatement. What happened in the activity of this project is the following. It was decided to modify a particular energy access portal and what occurred was an obstruction by the Orion DRA civilization.

Can you explain in more detail what the Orion DRA civilization is?

There have been two coinciding civilizations on your planet: Sirius and Orion DRA hybridization program. There was an initial cooperation with Orion DRA and there was a misappropriation of resources and a misdirection and misappropriation of the agreement. What developed next in the historical account was the permanent block and obstruction of the Sirius undertaking by the Orion DRA. Sirius hybrids that have been civilized on your planet were no longer permitted to leave via the gateway. There are Sirius hybrid Beings on your planet that have been effectively imprisoned by this dis-allegiance of Orion DRA.

How long have they been "imprisoned" on Earth?

The Sirius undertaking was permanently obstructed in 163 BC. At this point in your human time frame there was a turning point and we were no longer capable of instructing Sirius. They were no longer capable of continuing a project that would allow all the intergalactic alliances to once again use the gateway through the Orion Nebula.

How does this history tie in with the Pyramid history?

Sirius has not been a key player in the Pyramid origin theories, as many Human Beings believe. The Pyramids were in existence well before the Egyptian civilization took shape. The Pyramids predate by some margin the timeline that you have in your historical accounts. Sirius is not the same situation as the other Beings you refer to as "Extraterrestrials". Sirius is an isolated and exceptional divisive. We would like to correct specifically this situation, as the Sirius condition is separate and integral to your further understanding of time travel and the concept that you have of Heaven and Heaven's Gate.

What makes Sirius Beings an exceptional divisive?

Sirius hybrids have been in existence on your Earth density since the time period of 163 BC. You will need to reevaluate your historical accounts from this time period forward as the reason why you have many wars and unrest on your planet stem from this time period. The Beings from Sirius were once permitted to exist in the World of the Elohim. They have been sent specifically from this realm. Sirius is of a different makeup.

What historical account in 163 BC are you referencing?

The events of 163 BC are described in the biblical books you refer to as Maccabees 1 and 2.

NOTE: The Apocryphal books 1 and 2 of Maccabees recount the story of a Jewish revolt against the oppression of the Seleucid King, Antiochus IV Epiphanes. Judas Maccabeus led a successful revolt that lasted for 7 years and gave birth to the Jewish festival known as Hanukkah.

What exactly was Judas Maccabeus fighting for?

There was a decision that some would make the journey homeward and some would be remaining in the Earth plane. The Being Judas did not make the ascension experience. He along with a group of other Beings remained to help others contain an understanding and retrieve knowledge for a future ascension experience. Please be aware that Abraham returned in 163 BC for this purpose.

Abraham incarnated during this time?

The Being known as Abraham returned during this "period" to fulfill the Mission to bring the others home.

Did he reveal himself as Abraham or was he known as someone else?

He was Judas Maccabeus.

How can an ascended Being (Abraham) also incarnate?

Immortality and the ability to experience uninhibited time travel and connection with other worlds is an experience that a fully ascended Light Being will incorporate into further experience. Incarnation in this instance is not a reincarnation into a physical form.

Isn't that what incarnation is – taking on a physical form?

Energy can be contained within energy and with the description of Abraham reappearing in the guise of Judas Maccabeus, we are describing to you that there is a connection with the world and the intermediary world of Lyra. Judas Maccabeus is the template for Abraham's guidance.

Please simplify the concept of "energy being contained within energy".

Channeling is energy contained within energy. Just as you are utilizing us in this dialogue, so too was Abraham a guiding star for Judas Maccabeus.

You're saying that he was an energetic guide and not the continuing physical form of Judas.

This is a correct understanding. It is also why we describe Judas as having remained on the Earth plane.

This is not an easy idea for readers to absorb.

Your readership must be aware that this is a common occurrence throughout your linear history.

We read that Antiochus and a sect of Hellenized Jews were attempting to compromise traditional Jewish laws and were guilty of defiling the Temple and killing non-compliant Jews. What was the precise conflict?

The fight was a fight for the control of the gateway and the control of the knowledge. The factions between Judas and Antiochus are a similar experience to the Sinai experience. There is an ongoing obstruction to the gateway so that ascension is not an allowable ability or experience. The Beings that are continually trapped in the Earth plane existence that you are cooperating with and assisting in their journey homeward are all from the Sirius alliance.

Are Sirius Beings only represented through "Hebrew" people in today's world?

This is not accurate. "Hebrew" was a name given to the group that existed at that "time", as described in your biblical and historical accounts. Their religious affiliation to "Judaism" is something that was created over time as a tool to further derail these Beings from achieving ascension. Today there are Beings of Sirius origins across all religions, geographical regions and cultural designations.

To clarify, devotion to Judaism, Christianity, Islam or any other religion does not achieve ascension. Is that what you're saying?

Religious affiliation is a disruption in the ability to disseminate and share information. The information has not been hoarded by one particular group or religion. The information has been changed and confused so that some of you believe you understand the principles of immortality when in fact you do not.

The Bible references "Hebrews" and "Israelites". Are these terms interchangeable or is there an additional understanding we are not aware of?

The Hebrews are Beings who were able to make the step toward ascension in the Sinai experience. The Israelites are the Beings that have been left behind and have been given the tools but did not use them. There is a distinction between these two definitions. "Hebrews" is a definition that comes from the use of the codes of the letters known as Hebrew letters. The understanding that the letters are assembled for use in a language is not a correct belief.

128

The Hebrew letters were presented as codes for ascension and we turned them into a language for communication – is that what you're saying?

> This is correct. What has manifested is the use of a special string of codes for ascension reprogramming and now there is language that is being used and defining communication. The fall from Eden was the use of language as you are aware. The string of codes and letters that permitted Abraham to bring time travel and ascension awareness have been corrupted. The use is not for language in communication and physical speaking. The Israelite/Sirius connection is a project and a situation that continues today.

Did the Beings who were left behind take on the name "Israelite" as a reminder of the Sinai event and ascension? Is that why the name "Israel" has survived to present day?

> Nobody understands what happened and why they are doing what they are doing. The word and the experience have been perpetuated but the conscious understanding and knowing about the tools has been completely lost. This is like having a key for a vehicle that is instead being used as a doorstop. The term has been reimagined and the connection with the original experience has been lost. The dissemination of your book will create a foundation for those who are reconnecting with the ascension awareness. You will see, many will gravitate toward your preliminary explanation of what the term is. There is undoubtedly a need to further examine this term.

What if we are not modern day Hebrews or Israelis or don't practice Judaism? If the Reader is an Atheist from Germany or Czech Republic or a Hindu from India does that mean they don't have a Sirius connection or that this information does not apply to them?

> The understanding that these terms and Beings belong to the religious affiliation is not a correct explanation for your readership. Those who are not affiliated with the Abrahamic religions are not necessarily precluded from the description about the Sirius Beings.

Are you saying you can be anywhere in the world and still have a connection with the original meaning of the term "Israelite" or "Sirius"?

> This is correct. The confusion for your readers is that there are many Beings who were affiliated with the Sinai experience. Through the ages in the linear historical account, these Beings have gone off in different directions in terms of civilization and culture and religious organization.

The group we are calling "Israelites" were left behind or did not choose ascension and are now dispersed across the globe. The term Israelite does not simply refer to Beings who live in modern day Israel or who belong to this cultural group of humans. Is that an accurate summary?

> This is a correct understanding. What you refer to as the "lost tribes of Israel" are contained in the Earth plane. Many religious organizations originate from these Beings and do not realize their connection because of the seemingly different

organization and reorganization of their beliefs. The spread of peoples throughout the Earth plane occupying different lands has complicated this.

NOTE: It is written that ten of the original twelve tribes of Israel were "lost" or gradually assimilated into other peoples after the conquest of the Northern Kingdom by the Assyrians in 721 BC.

You are suggesting an almost entirely different meaning of Israel in this discussion.

Those Beings who say, "I have no connection with the Abrahamic religion and no connection with Judaism or Christianity or Islam" are also still possibly included in this description of Sinai, as the Beings were Beings of Sirius connection before the structure of organized religion was in existence. Religion is the reason why ascension has not occurred since the Sinai event. This recall will be a collapse in the worldwide beliefs of organized religion, primarily with the demise of Abrahamic religions. The collapse will also be permeating into other belief systems such as the questions about Hinduism and other religious organizations.

By "recall" are you referring to an upcoming ascension event?

This is correct. The global reorganization and the ascension event in the linear dates of 2034 to 2060 will affect all organized spiritual beliefs. You do not need to necessarily focus on the Abrahamic religion but this is certainly a good start as the majority of people who will be reading your book will be affiliated with these organizations.

Did these attempts to ascend and return home by Sirius Beings stir up envy in others? Is this the root of what we would call anti-Semitism?

> The distrust and animosity toward those Beings who are in connection fundamentally with the Sirius existence is the root of a lot of the discontent and problems in the Earth plane. It is not anti-Semitism that is at the root of the discontent. It is the ability of these Beings aligned with Sirius to return home to the immortal state.

Unconsciously we know that there are Beings (Sirius) who have access to other worlds, which in turn causes religious, political and social unrest in our societies. Is that accurate?

> What has occurred is simply the dynamics of the competitiveness for the ascension experience through the gateway. The obstruction of the gateway and the ascension experience for the Sirius Beings is the reason for the disruption in many of your religious factions, which has spilled over into your socio-political circles. Sirius Beings are effectively in a hostage state. The physical form is one level of their imprisonment. The obstruction of information has increased the amnesia so that the ascension experience has been almost completely forgotten.

Before you brought up 163 BC, you mentioned that Sirius Beings were once permitted in the World of the Elohim. Can you explain who or what Elohim is?

> We will achieve an understanding of the Elohim and their world in a further dissemination. It is best to

132

understand the Elohim as the Gatekeepers or Emissaries of a Realm that is beyond your galaxy. At this point in the discussion we advise that you return to the discussion of the pyramids.

Will you address the age of the pyramids?

The pyramids are of an ancient time lineage. The idea that they are correlated with the Egyptian civilization is incorrect. There is a Sumerian King who was an Elohim emissary who undertook a delivery on your planet. What had manifested in your historical accounts was an opportunity for a new alliance and allegiance. There were many who decided to align themselves with the Orion DRA agenda. This split into two different camps has existed for a very long time. The Sumerian King that we are referring to is aligned with the "Lemuria tale". When the accounts in your histories refer to Sumer they are actually referring to the Lemuria state. These two "civilizations" are one in the same.

NOTE: The Sumerians were a Mesopotamian civilization, present day Iraq. According to historians they predate the Egyptians and Greeks and are believed to be the first known complex human civilization dated ca. 4000 BC. Their religion described "Sky Gods" descending and ruling over their people.

You've said that Lemuria is not a "geographical location" or "civilization". Why are you referring to it as such now?

Your current understanding is a belief that there was a people and place called Lemuria. Lemuria is not a civilization. This reference is to correct your

current understanding. When your histories speak of
"Lemuria" they are in actuality referencing Sumer.
Sumer was a civilization that had achieved the
Lemuria state. This is the confusion for many of
you.

Are historians lacking the evidence or are they modifying
history?

There has been a repeated reforming of history in
your written tablets and later books. The Sumerian
history you are in possession of today is not the
original story. Refer to this as Lemuria for this
discussion. What occurred during this Lemuria state
was a sonic attack and a flooding of the density with
a hyper sonic instability. The Orion DRA gateway
was obstructed at this point and those Beings in the
Lemuria state were not able to construct a project so
that they could save themselves.

Was this Lemuria state/Sumer the time period when the
pyramids were built?

The pyramid idea was created during this "time".
The pyramids were not built by the Egyptians or the
Sumerians. The pyramids were built by Beings that
were of epic stature compared to the current stature
of Beings on your planet. These Beings will be
discussed in a further dissemination. The purpose of
the pyramids was an alignment with the Star Gate
that is obstructed. The alignment with the Star Gate
was not an example to signal to us or to send a
communication or create energy systems as you
have hypothesized.

What exactly was the purpose of the pyramids, in simpler terms?

> The pyramids were created as recognition of an event where we once had control of the gateway and of your universe. The pyramids are a symbolic construction. They are not a tomb or a storehouse or a vehicle to manufacture energy. The pyramids were simply a symbolic tribute to our breakthrough as we had overcome an obstacle that we wanted to mark with great celebration. You continue in your own civilization to mark holidays and events and award those achievements. This is a similar concept in that we "landed" and had created an indestructible and impermeable fortress and our once formidable activities are commemorated with these structures. There is nothing more to the purpose of the pyramids.

People have spent their lives theorizing about the pyramids and the technologies that built them. What you're saying sounds both facile and crazy.

> We find it inconceivable that there are hundreds of theories and discussions about how these structures were created or built. The stone work that you have examined and reexamined and researched and calculated was in fact moved by Beings who were epic in stature and had the energy resources to create such structures.

You previously stated that the sands were "moved" during the building of the pyramids. Now you're saying large Beings built them.

135

There were very large Beings that once occupied your planet, specifically during the Lemuria state. The stones and sands that make up the structure were moved via sonic capability. This is not what you would call "pseudo science". Your "acoustic levitation" theories are somewhat similar to the abilities we are describing. We do not recommend discussing these Beings at great length until further understanding is acquired.

If the pyramids at Giza aren't Egyptian in origin why are they in present day Egypt?

The location of the civilization during the Lemuria state is not anywhere near the present location of the pyramids. There was a monumental shift of the tectonic plates of your planet. The pyramids are not presently in their original position. The deluge that occurred during Lemuria created an unusual shift on the planet and there was a grandiose shifting of the tectonic plates and the pyramids were under water. What we want you to understand is that there was a shift over time. The pyramids have been submerged more than once. There has been more than one flood in the history of Earth during the time of Sirius and the Sirius hybrid occupation.

This is a lot for anyone to absorb.

There will be further discussion about the pyramids. Do not believe that creating theories or inventing scientific explanations will allow you to ascend and exit through a gateway that has been obstructed for too long now. Once your DNA coding strings are reformed you will no longer have a desire to explain all these existing theories and theories about theories. You will have a desire to explore new worlds and a desire to master the time travel continuum and paradigm.

What you're telling us and suggesting is that our documented history is almost completely wrong. People reading this will either dismiss it or become depressed.

When Man Being accepts that the world has been shaped by historical inaccuracies of epic proportions then you will be more equipped and able to absorb coding and frequency strings. Your DNA will be modified so that you will no longer be restricted to your form. You are all trapped in your form and this condition will not change with your slow and inaccurate scientific discoveries and hypotheses. There is often a personal agenda to correlate a theory with the finding. This does not advance your understanding of the truth.

Have any of our documented civilizations led a fully successful ascension?

The civilizations that have occurred on your planet have all failed in one respect. There are not many Man Being candidates who have access through their own gateway portals. You have a small number of Ascended Masters and this is a staggering inequality and what we would suggest is ineffectual. When you create the conditions so that all of you

137

become Ascended Masters then there will be a difference in your activities on your planet. We would like you all to reject these inaccurate beliefs and make a stand against the Orion DRA obstruction. We would like you to make your way to your own individual gateways.

11

Gateways and Belief

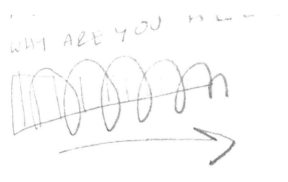

You've mentioned that we need to make our way through our own "individual gateways". Can you clarify what a gateway is?

> There has been a "recent" event of a collapse of infrastructure, which you refer to as the Notre Dame Cathedral. This event will assist in your understanding of the gateway.

NOTE: The Notre Dame is a 12th century Cathedral in Paris, France. On April 15th 2019 a fire broke out beneath the roof, destroying it along with the spire and the upper walls of the Church. Investigations have concluded that the fire was caused by a "renovation mishap".

What does this fire have to do with ascension or gateways?

> The allowance of the collapse of infrastructure is an understanding that what unites your awareness with your existence in the Earth plane is an appreciation and respect of form. The form is assembled in a belief structure.

Form is a belief stream. Is that what you're saying?

> Yes. When there is belief of form there is form. The gateway of consciousness and the gateway of reconnection for your own individual ascension experience is an undertaking in reformatting your beliefs and forming beliefs. As you are forming beliefs you are forming your Light Body and the awareness of the Light Body and the connections are the connections in experience.

Are you saying that our beliefs activate a gateway?

140

A gateway is a measure of ascension belief. You contain a gateway in the assembly of your Light Being. Your Light Being is assembled in a gateway or a belief system. Gateway and belief are one and the same. The gateway to ascension through the belief in ascension is one and the same. The change in the belief structure in the Earth plane system and dynamic is a collapse in a gateway of belief. The gateway of belief is a gateway that you are reassembling and also collapsing.

Please explain what you mean by "reassembling and collapsing".

When you express the understanding that things may no longer exist, this is a collapse of a belief. From this collapse you reassemble a new belief.

Most people would understand "gateway" as a manifested portal, which we pass through. The idea that our beliefs are gateways is profound.

"Belief" and "gateway" are synonymous. Please explain this to your readers so they understand that the current belief and the current gateway is your own expressed gateway. When things collapse and no longer hold value for you individually, you begin ascension. What is unique in this ascension experience and undertaking is your interconnection with your soul group. Those Beings who are in existence in form with you will also join you in the ascension experience.

If we all have these interconnected "soul groups" that are ascending with us, can we create a global shift even if everyone isn't consciously trying to ascend?

> This is somewhat the case. The understanding that the monumental shift in energy and shift in beliefs en masse can cause a splitting and shift from the matrix and construct of your organized belief is a correct understanding.

Is that why you referred to the Notre Dame fire at the beginning of this discussion?

> This is precisely the reason. The forms and physicality and objects that contain your world and ideologies are no longer needed in the ascension experience and the moment that the belief in a new awareness is fulfilled the form no longer exists.

This could be a frightening thought for the Reader.

> We appreciate the concern in this respect but the fundamental ties that organize belief systems like Religion and Government and Finance are no longer a truth that is needed. There is a collapse of the world organization and the collapse is equivalent to what is disseminated in the biblical accounts of a "flood".

Are you saying that the true cause of the Notre Dame fire was our change in a belief system?

> A massive shift and change is on the horizon as the horizon of your beliefs is coinciding with a new awareness and undertaking. Please do not present

these ideas in a way that is inciting others to act irresponsibly. The collapse of the Notre Dame is properly understood as a "spontaneous implosion" and not a random act of what you would call "arson" or "terror".

If changing a belief system causes "spontaneous implosions", why was the Notre Dame fire the only event? Wouldn't every church in the world simultaneously implode if the belief systems were changing?

This is an interesting question. The unified response and change in belief is not presently in the construct of change. The example of the Notre Dame and the implosion at this place and space in our understanding during the dissemination of these ideas is not equivalent to the global acceptance of change.

Can there be a unified global collapse of infrastructure?

Yes. If there is a global acceptance of change of belief you will be experiencing in unison, a collapse. It is not synchronized. This will be shifting. You will be experiencing more events of this nature, such as the Notre Dame cathedral fire and there will be more events and devastations that occur as the reorganization of belief is unfolding on a global scale.

We don't want readers to take this as permission to set fire to buildings or harm anyone.

Your readers must understand that doing harm to each other is not a path to enlightenment and does

143

not achieve ascension. The intentional destruction of a structure is also not a pathway to ascension. Setting fire to a building or seeking to destroy it forcefully is not a decision that is in alignment with the Repair Project.

You've mentioned the biblical account of a "flood". Was there a rescue of Beings during that "catastrophe"?

The Earth plane existence is an example of a rescue mission and the Beings who are contained in the Earth plane are all Beings who have been rescued from the cataclysmic events you are inquiring about. Please understand that the situation in the Earth plane existence is a rescue mission but you are being kept and obstructed from leaving through ascension, as the Orion DRA agenda requires you to occupy space. The events are now unfolding however and the world that has previously been occupied by Orion DRA is no longer available to them, as Man Being is returning home.

You're saying that as Man Being prepares for ascension, structures will continue to spontaneously implode. Is this occurring simply because we are shifting our beliefs systems en masse?

Yes. There are other events where there will be automatic and spontaneous implosion and seemingly external causes for destruction. What we are witnessing are the energy folds collapsing. Your thoughts hold form in place and they can also collapse it. We urge you to recreate your stories so that the containment in the Earth plane that you are currently all experiencing will once and for all be lifted.

12

The Disconnect

You've suggested that we "recreate our stories" so that we can return home. We have no greater story than our belief in an afterlife.

> Please recall our discussion about involuntary disconnect and voluntary disconnect. Involuntary disconnect is equal to your experience of "death". Your notion of an afterlife is connected to this choice.

Akhenaten chose to voluntarily disconnect which means he understood that he is immortal. Involuntary means we don't have complete awareness and we "wait for death to arrive" via illness or circumstance. Correct?

> Yes. What is encouraging for your Reader is that even "after death" you are presented with a choice. This choice is a commitment to restore what was once for all of us. There is a choice to permanently live in Light and to access the World of Immortality. Unfortunately Man Being is experiencing a continued obstruction of this gateway. We aim to provide a solution to remedy the obstruction.

Who specifically is the cause for this obstruction?

> Orion DRA.

Can you elaborate some more on the Orion DRA?

> Orion DRA or DRA as we refer to this group, are Beings from the Orion Star System. This is not a benevolent cause.

Is this group currently trying to prevent us from ascension?

The activity of the DRA agenda and Man Being's consumption is furthering the obstruction to the gateway. When you turn to religious agenda in an attempt to have access to the "afterlife" the difficulty for many of you is that you are not reversing your consumptive ways. Consumption and the addictions that you all suffer from are DRA agenda and DRA devices to maintain control over the gateway.

That sounds disparaging.

It is a problem that we cannot correct easily. We may continue sending out transmissions en masse but if Man Being does not commit and ask for further modification then we cannot assist. This dialogue will disseminate knowledge that will inspire people to commit and request modification and acceptance of code. It seems highly simplistic that all one has to do is ask but this is the truth of the situation that is easily overlooked.

It is extremely disparaging to think that there are other Beings like DRA that are influencing or manipulating our behaviour.

Do not focus on other Beings. Commit yourselves to the change and you will be free from this containment.

What exactly does "committing to the change" entail?

It is necessary that you no longer focus on consumptive activity and harming others. Addiction and consumption and these activities are self-perpetuating and pushing you into a state that will not heal the DNA codes that we wish to modify.

You refer to your existence as "a mess" and we must agree with this description. With this transmission, we are not able to repair you en masse. It is requiring individuals to come forth and accept and ask for the codes. This book is achieving a reconnection of Beings. We have sent out transmissions en masse that have been received by many but they do not ask for further modification.

Why don't they ask for further modification?

Man Being has been educated in such a way that you do not ask for things that are obvious. When you say the phrase "build it and we will come" this is an obvious truth. You have been advised to work very hard and achieve goals that are in some cases unachievable and put you in a further perpetuation of consumptive madness. Asking for code and further modification is not consumption and a very simple and profound choice.

When someone experiences an involuntary disconnect or "death", can they still choose to ascend further or do they have to reincarnate?

There is still an option to ascend. You can once again permanently exist in Lightness. This can be achieved. There is a reality where no conflict or distress exists. There is a reality in which we will all experience peace. Please allow yourselves the opportunity and continue in your modification.

Is this peaceful existence that you're describing aligned with what we believe is "Heaven"?

The afterlife is not a reward. Heaven is not a reward for good behaviour and upholding a strict belief system. Man Being's understanding of "Heaven" is a subscription to the Judgment paradigm.

What exactly occurs after an involuntarily disconnect?

You are presented with an opportunity to return home.

Why then are Beings choosing to reincarnate?

Those Beings that are not accepting modification are vulnerable during this experience and may resume their continued existence in the reincarnation cycle. This is a DRA construct. Those that are directed back to the Earth plane will continue another cycle and will be able to modify further but will still have to go through a long process.

We understand that this is part of the obstruction but what is the main reason Beings are choosing reincarnation over the World of Immortality or Light?

You are led to believe that you cannot "be" with each other unless it is on the Earth density. This is not the case.

We panic because we want to see our loved ones again. Is that all?

You do not have an understanding of what "modification" and "ascension" mean. You choose reincarnation because you believe it offers you what you know – a return to your "family". There is however a way to both ascend and be with your family. The Beings that you are able to communicate with now and feel a comradery with will likely be the Beings that you will interact with again in a different form. This is related to our discussion about your "soul ascension group". Earth is not the only existence. Your family is not confined to Earth.

Why are these DRA Beings doing this? How does our presence on Earth benefit them?

Your physical presence creates a sonic disturbance that blocks the gateway and free flowing Light Travel throughout the universe. This is a complex discussion that we will return to. For now, the understanding that your physical presence allows these Beings to control gateway allowance is sufficient.

This sounds like we are making fear-based decisions even in "death".

The choice to return to the Earth plane is a choice that is manifested in fear, as we have already discussed the Judgment experience. When there is fear, there is fear-based decision making and when there is fear-based decision making there is an effort to direct these Beings back to Earth, as organized by the Orion DRA capture. We will discuss the Judgment experience in a further dissemination. For now, the question of why some have fear or fears when they exit the Earth density experience is very simple to explain.

What is the simple explanation?

> Some of you simply do not understand or appreciate that there is modification and that there is time travel and that there is an experience that will lead you to your ultimate blueprint and further your existence in a fully functioning stream of dimensions.

Is not knowing or accepting that there is something beyond Earth the root problem?

> Those who are leaving their Earth density form with many unanswered questions are inclined to make rash and ineffectual decisions. Understanding that there are other options that are available will help you to continue the ascension experience when you are presented with a choice in the "Afterlife".

Is it fair to suggest that our religions have not prepared us for this choice?

> Your religions have unfortunately created a circular capture whereby Man Being believes that its only options are "Heaven" and "Hell". The decision to embrace ascension or continue your ascension experience out of form is easy once you have some understanding that there are further options. We will discuss these options in another dialogue. Your readers must first absorb the tools for ascension.

152

If the Reader ultimately dismisses the information in this book will they still have an opportunity to modify?

> Simply being exposed to this dialogue may trigger the realization that you do have options, when faced with the decision. Some of you will make a very last minute and surprised decision to continue your ascension when presented with these options simply because you read this passage. Those who are faced with the decision and do not have the informational tools to make an informed and correct choice will resume their Earth density experience.

Something isn't making sense in this explanation. Why are so many people incarnating on Earth if all it takes is some slight exposure to these ideas?

> The primary reason is that disseminated information has so rarely reached you without an immediate effort to intercept and conceal it. The Orion DRA capture is designed to make reincarnation look like the easy choice. On Earth you do not need to do anything spectacular and this is the place that is familiar to you. When faced with these decisions, if one is not informed about the other options, then the easy way to proceed would be to re-embrace the capture and this is understandable.

Essentially, whether the Reader believes this or not, it will serve them when the "time" comes.

> Dissemination is effective even if it is not initially thought highly of or regarded as truth. The

dissemination is something that will be utilized when those Beings are being faced with the decision.

There are people who claim to have "Near Death Experiences", aka NDEs. What they are experiencing?

What the NDE is describing is a change in the belief of the participant and the understanding that you can change your belief even in the full experience of an involuntary disconnect.

Why do they return to Earth if they've changed their beliefs? The Beings who turn back and reenter the physical form do so with a new understanding and the need to disseminate. These Beings are committed to disseminating the belief that immortality is available for you even upon an involuntary disconnect experience.

There are several books and movies written about the NDE experiences but our notion of the afterlife hasn't changed much.

The understanding of instruction is not complete. There is not a complete account that exists in your popular written accounts of what to expect and how to conduct oneself during the disconnect. What is not clear is how to change the belief if you do not experience this "tunnel of light" for yourself.

There is mass confusion about the "tunnel and the light" description.

We have already determined with you that our presence in the perceived tunnel and experience of travel is creating the white light experience. Once Beings experience the involuntary disconnect they are immediately in the presence of an assembly of Light Beings. The decision to join our assembly is a correct choice if one is interested and committed to the immortal stream of existence.

You have emphasized the importance of a voluntary disconnect throughout the dialogue. Are you now suggesting that the opportunity to ascend is still available to those Beings who involuntarily disconnect?

We have said there is opportunity to reformulate your belief in an involuntary disconnect. The point of your work and dissemination is to discourage those who are relying on understanding the instruction in the involuntary experience, as there is opportunity for an incorrect experience and an incorrect belief map of awareness.

Readers are best to choose the voluntary disconnect because the involuntary experience might present some obstacles if they are not properly prepared. Is that accurate?

This is correct. While the voluntary disconnect is preferred, it is still possible to choose ascension during the involuntary disconnect experience. Please urge your readers to commit to the voluntary disconnect.

Those Beings who choose the voluntary disconnect do not have to endure this same experience. Is that correct?

Yes. For those who voluntarily disconnect, there is no need to choose a direction or a tunnel or perceive a correct operation of instruction or a priority of instructions. You are automatically joining an assembly, an assembly of experience – a path to the World of Immortality.

Can there be a situation whereby a Being chooses the voluntary disconnect but dies before the ascension is achieved?

In some cases an involuntary disconnect experience occurs even though the intention to make the full ascension is in place. There are situations that are sometimes not preventable and the discourse in this dialogue is essential to prepare those who are accidently making an involuntary disconnect for whatever reason.

The "tunnel" experience sounds like an instruction. Is that what it is?

The tunnel or the perceived tunnel of light is an instruction as there are Beings that you are encountering in this experience. They are from our world and our assembly. There is a unique alignment whereby Beings who have made an involuntary disconnect are sometimes assembled in this experience you are calling the tunnel and are waiting to make a connection with other members of your soul group of ascension. The tunnel of light as you are aware, is an experience where there are many of us in this space and place and the perception of the white light is the result.

Are NDE accounts an attempt to inform Man Being of specific instructions?

156

The NDE dissemination is a wake up call for others to be prepared. There is a loss in the dissemination account, as it is not clearly explained. There is no real understanding of what to do. All that is being described is that there is an experience and an experience of Beings that are forming the white light.

It seems like NDE accounts have largely failed at disseminating the truth.

It is important to understand that the NDE is an opportunity and a final chance to recreate a new belief stream.

How many people are having NDEs?

The NDE is something that occurs more frequently than is documented, as there are many Beings who are encountering a leave of form. Some refer to this as "astral travel" and some refer to this as "out of body" in dream state. There is a frequent occurrence of an involuntary disconnect during the sleep state.

Are you saying that we don't have to be sick or injured to have the NDE? An involuntary disconnect can occur while we sleep/dream. Is that correct?

There are many of you who are passing between the two states of form and the state of ascension in your dream state and are not aware. Many of you are entering an involuntary disconnect experience where you do return with an enlightened understanding about death and the ascension

157

journey. Some of you equate this with a "profound dream" but you are not attributing it to an involuntary disconnect.

What is causing us to have dreams?

The need for you to align yourselves with the ascension experience is requiring you to leave the experience of the physical form state. In the dream state the function of your existence shifts into a slightly different frequency of existence that is more equivalent to a disconnect state. Sleep is practice for a disconnect awareness state.

What do you recommend we do after we have these profound dreams or astral travel experiences?

The recommendation is to consider the importance of sleep and a sleep state. Many of you are deprived of an essential amount of sleep. Sleep is not to regenerate the physical form. It is to give yourself enough ascension ground and experience.

Are we downloading ascension information in our sleep state?

This is correct. The experience of ascension and the disconnect state affects you in your physical form. If you are not nurturing the disconnect state you are not furthering your ascension ability. You must further your belief in the voluntary disconnect. You will find that those Beings who are choosing the voluntary disconnect will make a concerted effort to achieve as much sleep as they can master.

Are relaxation and meditation aligned with this understanding? Is meditation equivalent to "nurturing the disconnect state"?

> This is not accurate. It is the REM frequency in the dream state that is equivalent to the disconnect state.

If Man Being is trapped how are we still able to access this state? Why wouldn't Orion DRA obstruct this as well?

> There was no ability to completely contain and imprison the experience of those Beings entrapped in form in the Earth plane density. The light and the light assembly experience is a powerful and formidable experience that cannot ever be completely contained or confined. This is the only thing that allows your belief to continue onward and recreate the Light Being embodiment.

The Earth plane seems a torturous place by that description.

> It is just a fact that there is no imprisonment or ability or anything that can completely contain the light and for this reason you are suffering even more than you know. If you did not have the ability to reconnect with the experience that you are designed for there would be no need to try to reach for something better and higher in your experience. The complete containment of light is unachievable. It has never been achieved.

Will we receive the full instruction on what to do during an involuntary disconnect experience?

Your readers will of course require a management and a new plan and a map of awareness. This instruction will be shared as we further along in your dissemination. The reason we are not emphasizing the instruction at this place and space is to encourage your readers to subscribe to the voluntary disconnect path, as this path is the preferred journey of ascension. There will be further instruction for your readership in subsequent disseminations.

13

Misunderstandings

We've spoken about instructions and how to navigate the NDE. In the 1970s there was a cult known as "Heaven's Gate". They were known for their strange practices, including mass suicide. What can you tell us about this event and the instructions this group received?

What has repeatedly occurred in a cult or cult organization is a supreme misunderstanding of our instruction. Those that take the initial transmission and then proceed to undertake leadership without responsibility achieve nothing in the end except further misunderstanding. Man Being has lacked the stamina to continue to modify awareness and achieve supreme understanding. When you only undertake after the first step then you are left with an incomplete dialogue and result. We have repeatedly assisted and continue to assist. The choice to sustain and allow further modification is yours.

Were the meticulous practices of the Heaven's Gate cult a misinterpretation of instruction? What caused them to behave this way?

NOTE: The cult was known for practicing a strict diet, abstaining from sex, castration and mass suicide.

We have defined our requirements when we communicate. There has been an unfortunate misinterpretation of our intended advice and love and support. There is a requirement when we extend our help and that is that you must please listen. There are some practices that may benefit and further your listening and absorption skills. It is never our advice however, to commit suicide or to do physical harm to others. Suicide is not a pathway to immortality. Your readership must be aware of this.

Why do people veer so far from the instruction?

There is a lack of patience. Unfortunately the modification requires many steps and if you could modify so that our directives were completely absorbed in an instance this would certainly help. The difficulty that we are encountering is simply that the communication and modifications cannot reach you succinctly due to your consumptive habits. This is perpetuating a sonic disturbance and until this is managed more effectively modification will need to continue in phases.

Was the modification process always this way?

No. There was a time in your current civilization when modification could be absorbed instantly. There are accounts of those who received messages from "God" and "visions" and "Prophets". These accounts are somewhat accurate. There have been opportunities to assist and achieve full modification but being incomplete, Man Being has distorted the information as well as the feeling.

Why are you using terms like "incomplete"? How can an individual become complete if there is no end to existence?

The term "incomplete" is in reference to those who wish to continue in their free form involvement in the universe. This Repair Project is a joint collaboration and the sooner we are all involved

163

together the sooner we will reestablish free involvement and free experience. Please relay this information.

Humans aren't typically great at being collaborative.

That belief is collapsing. There is also a misunderstanding that Man Being must wait to be retrieved and reunited with his "true self" and true condition. We require you to agree to continue doing the work that is necessary for the benefit of all. The reason for all the visitation and "sightings" is that we are all in this together.

At times it sounds like humans are dragging everyone else down. We're keeping the Light Beings and Light Workers busy.

There is a basic belief that an outside force will guide you to safety. That an outside force will change your life and that an external experience will benefit Mankind. The changes that are occurring for some are minute modifications in the grand scheme of things. We do not regard Man Being as an inconvenience. We would like to assist you and in turn we would like your assistance. These ideas that you are abhorrent and an obtrusion and a responsibility are not precisely correct. Many Beings have modification that is needed and you will all once again be one and the same.

What restrictions do Light Beings have and what will our modification accomplish for them?

You believe that you occupy space. In fact you occupy sound and this sound is not the sound that you naturally make. When we together signal and sound in our precise and correct frequency alignment then the gateway will open once again. We ask that you continue your dialogue with us and allow yourself to further absorb understanding and frequency. The sonic obtrusion and distortion is making you very tired and this is the main reason why we are not having a higher success in helping Man Being to further modulate and understand. Please continue the dialogue.

What happens if we don't continue?

There are many who stop at this point and then information that is incomplete is disseminated and you perpetuate the problem. There are many in your Earth plane that are disseminating incomplete information and beliefs. This is not entirely a fault of their own. Your condition in your density is not an easy one. We ask those who have the stamina to continue the modification. There are far too many of you now pedaling outdated beliefs that will no longer assist you, albeit with good intention.

Do we continue modification by asking questions?

You are receiving codes and transmission especially during your sleep. When you upload information via asking a question, you then allow absorption of codes and frequencies that are previously unavailable to you. We are not "abducting" and forcing decisions on you. We are prepared to share codes and are continuing to send transmission but if

165

the transmission cannot be absorbed completely then we are at a loss. Please continue your dialogue and allow the modification that will benefit Man Being. There is no incorrect question. If you have a question then you have the answer. This is the way that it works.

Are you capable of entering our density or atmosphere without issue or do you use protective devices of any kind?

There are "devices" that some "extraterrestrials" are able to use to propel themselves through densities and energetic fields. If you consider that a garment is something that you wear to achieve stability whether it is body temperature or comfort such as protection from extreme climate and variation in climate you will understand that in order for us to execute propulsion through your density and densities in the Earth dimension, we must calibrate and recalibrate. This is not always achievable with our allowances.

Why is that?

The gateway that we would like to have continued access through is not available, as we have informed you in previous discussion. Our entry into your dimension and axis is not the most protected avenue.

Are what we call "spaceships" also devices that you use?

We are able to envelop our Being in a way that travel is possible. The shape that you are experiencing or perceiving as a "spaceship" is a manifestation of the point of entry and also the point of exit. The angle and the timing of entry will dictate a shape, for example circular or triangular. As we achieve equilibrium in your electro magnetic field we must calibrate and this will produce a different shape on the horizon. Entry for us involves a three-step procedure and this will expand and contract and allow a shape that is elliptical and flat.

What is the "three-step" procedure?

When we are able to communicate and enter your dimension the shape that will initially appear to you is elliptical and very flattened. The three-step process for entry into your Earth density involves a change in our energy field so that we initially enter as a frequency of light. This then will transform into a more solid form and then a more gaseous state when we exit. The three part process allows us to quickly enter and exit for the purpose of taking measurement and observing the conditions and repositioning to prepare for our strategic gateway alliance mission.

The Repair Project, in other words.

Yes. There are many Beings now that are making visitation in preparation of the Repair Project. Visitation will reach an unprecedented number in 2019, your time. The crystalline or crystal appearance of some Beings is a result of the change in the polarity redirection of their cellular structure as they enter your dimension. They have learned how to create a protective shell. This is something that Man Being will be able to achieve when we once again have a functioning gateway allowance and we prepare to modify further.

Are you saying that Man Being will be able to naturally create a protective shell or protective aura or field for inter-dimensional time travel?

Yes. Once Man Being is modified and restored to the original state, you will be able to change form. This will allow a change in state and a protection allowance for travel.

Does the protective layer automatically form once you travel to the Earth density or to different atmospheres?

We do not have a condition where we need to think about being. We adjust to our circumstances. This is something that Man Being is not able to do. When we continue with modification you will be able to achieve this and not have to prepare or "think" about it. Your existence is limited to your fate on Earth. When we continue to modify you, your existence will be whole and there will not be a limitation and a requirement for you to exist in a particular state. In order to travel and experience other worlds you will be able to change your form. This will be a natural condition and not something that you need to learn or teach yourself how to do. If you consider the octopus and your questions from a previous dialogue, this Being has mastery and is able to make the changes that we speak about in this dialogue. It is this ability that you will be equipped with.

Humans have had difficulty describing their encounters with Light Beings. Is it because these Beings are formless?

Your ability to understand and see and feel other Beings in their multistate function will be restored. When Man Being speaks about "green aliens" or "blue" or "purple" or "grey", this is a limited awareness. They are not a single color or a singular shape. This is dependent on where they are in the moment. Man Being sees them as a specific color and in a certain form. While this is true for your experience in the Earth dimension it is not true for other densities or places. Your limited understanding will be repaired as the modification and modulation continues. The "spaceship" is in fact similar to the shape we have previously discussed.

Do you mean the tetrahedron?

Correct. This experience is something that we would ask you to continue to absorb. The shape when compressed is more elliptical and flattened. We are using basic terms with you so you do not become overwhelmed with the technology.

So if we saw you coming in through the sky you would appear to us as what we call "UFOs" or "spaceships" but you're actually a tetrahedron?

Correct. If you consider the tetrahedron shape, this shape is a way for you to prepare to exist in a

169

different energy state. While we do not have to study and practice how to achieve a change in our state this is an exercise for now that we would request you to manage. If you consider yourself standing in the complete shape you will further your absorption of these concepts.

If you don't need a craft to travel then what crashed at Roswell?

There are experimental projects and alliances with governmental agencies and organizations on your planet. These achievements continue and the technology and development continues. The crash is correct. There is evidence and there are witnesses and information is available. The question one may need to ask is, "Was this craft strictly Extraterrestrial in origin or is this a collaborative and exhaustive activity?" The machine or machinery is not an application that we require to travel but the technologies that you continue to develop through archaic means certainly can achieve goals, albeit not happy ones. There are continued elaborate alliances ongoing. We are not involved in these activities.

What is your main involvement?

Our responsibilities are to help those who choose to continue to achieve the modification that will allow your ascended awareness. As you have already discovered, ascension is not a modification of spiritual "thinking" or spirituality. There are practical applications and your limitations, with respect to spiritual understanding, are now required to shift. There was a time when the heightened

170

spiritual awareness was important and the elevated feelings assisted us in our modification. This application is no longer as beneficial and we are requiring a more serious attitude and responsibility.

Are powerful organizations also shifting their attitudes? The Vatican under Pope Francis stated, when asked, that they would baptize Extraterrestrials and that there is in fact no Hell. They have since denied these statements, of course. Is this the beginning of a new epoch for the Vatican and are they preparing for a paradigm shift?

They will require help from Light Beings. Should warfare escalate they will require negotiation and representatives from these worlds to meet with organizations on your planet. We are not involved in the politics but are aware of the undertakings and the requirements that the Vatican upholds. Should there be a need for a new ideology they will soon turn to a new attitude and seek a protective alliance. The Vatican is fully aware of the experiences that Man Being has had with Light Beings and the continued experiences. When it comes to a question of full disclosure you will be undoubtedly surprised at the outcome. When there is a need for protective alliance then you will soon see how quickly the truth is revealed. The Vatican is fully aware of the modification project that has begun.

Is that why Pope Benedict retired?

There are two streams of "thought" in the Vatican and some members are aligned with those organizations that have allegiance to activities such as Roswell. The Vatican is turning a new leaf and

171

there is a Reformation in progress, yes. The Being known as Pope Benedict has an allegiance with those organizations that are not working to create a free and happy Earth experience.

We'd like to end this particular discussion by addressing any recommended habits for those seeking modification.

Consuming energy is not required. Preserving energy is the achievement we would like to assist you with. The consumptive pattern is not aligned with your re-connective healing. What we require you to do is as little as possible. Man Being is presently wired to do as much as possible and this has translated and manifested into a consumptive madness.

What specifically are we doing that you are labeling as "consumptive madness"?

Whether it is eating or drinking or spending or addiction or sex or exercise or overthinking, Man Being is applying himself in such a way that healing is not allowed to exist. We request you to be good to yourself and use reasonable judgment. Specifically, alcohol is not a correct pattern for your re-connective feeling. Please exercise caution. The energy patterns that alcohol creates are disruptive to the re-connective healing.

That will not be a popular recommendation.

The patterning or energy patterns created by alcohol consumption are not aligned with the healing that needs to exist. If you would like to call this pineal gland decalcification or repair then please proceed with this line of reasoning. The issue is specifically the energy field or pattern that alcohol will create. Alcohol has had a disruptive pattern and is not a tool for an ascended Being.

Yet wine has been mentioned as something sacred in Scripture and Mythology. Even certain hallucinogens have been said to be gateways to heightened perception.

We are not criticizing the use of plant or psychedelics. We are speaking of alcohol.

How about some food items?

What will assist your modification is plant based and not heated or fermented or distorted.

So raw fruits and vegetables is what you're describing?

This is appropriate.

Are you suggesting that we adhere to this strict diet?

At this stage in your modification, a restriction on food and a food list is not necessary but will assist you further if you wish to comply with a more energized way of eating.

What specific capabilities will we achieve with the modification through this dialogue and commitment?

Your hearing will improve. Your ability to feel the meaning will improve and this is what we indicate by the word hearing. Imagine a flat grid and an

173

image of twisting the grid the way you twist a towel to wring it. This is related to your DNA. You are reforming another strand of DNA.

With that new strand, what will the capabilities be?

You will be able to have a physical contact experience with us.

14

The Luminaries

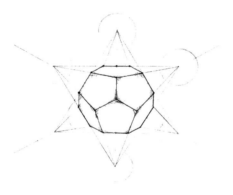

We've spoken about Light and the Light Body assembly in this dialogue but we haven't discussed the sources of Earth's light. What is our relationship with the luminaries (Sun, Moon, stars) in our solar system?

We would like to return to the prophecy you are referring to as "Five Hundred, Ten and Five". There is a Being known as Masha'Allah who existed in the time period 500 years before Dante's written work.

NOTE: The individual being referenced is Masha'Allah ibn Athari. He was a leading Astrologer and Astronomer of the 8th century AD in what is modern day Iraq. He was born in 740 and died c. 815 AD.

What can you tell us about Masha'Allah?

The luminaries that he calculated created a new understanding that was not absorbed and was not credited correctly. There is a book in particular that he has written that has not been fully credited to him. Please correct this. Masha'Allah's concepts on the luminaries expand the idea that the Light is available for all.

Which book of his are you referring to?

The work is known under a Latin title "Liber de Orbe". This was a later translation of the work.

What exactly did Masha'Allah's work contribute?

The position of the luminaries can be equated with the understanding of the light and how bringing the light into your life is the ultimate benefit to Mankind. His understanding that you are in control of your own destiny remains a threatening belief.

Can you elaborate on what Masha'Allah means by "position of the Luminaries"?

The way that you subscribe to and encounter the luminaries is a construct of your belief system of the day. He introduced a new way of seeing and understanding the luminaries that was controversial and beneficial for Western civilization but not a benefit to his own culture and society. This knowledge was seen as controversial and was appropriated by the Byzantine Emperor known as Leo IV for his own use. This Emperor also misinterpreted the work to further control the masses. There is an understanding in Masha'Allah's writing that ascension is achievable.

Was he suggesting that humans could "position" or control the luminaries?

You will understand and fully acknowledge that you do not wait for the luminaries, for example the Sun, to move around your lives. You in fact move around the luminaries in unison. There is an experience where you become luminaries and contribute and coincide with this experience that you are asking about.

How do we "become luminaries"?

This experience coincides with a new understanding of Astronomy. It proposes that the energy that is created from the ascension awakening and experience will shift the position and movement of those objects that you are staring at in the sky. This is what Masha'Allah was teaching.

Is this like saying that our Light Body reassembly or ascension contributes to what we observe in the sky?

There is a new awareness that you become luminaries and that you are luminaries. Your position and situation is such that you also have a map and a movement that is calculated by the number of Beings who make ascension.

Does this mean that the orbit of the Sun and Moon are not fixed?

Yes. The luminaries are not on fixed trajectories. They can be manipulated and changed. There is a monumental release of energy that is created during a mass ascension experience that will shift the position of the luminaries' orbit and axes. This creates unprecedented experiences on the Earth plane that Man Being will attribute to "God's Hand", when in fact it is your own hands who have participated in the change.

What is most important to absorb from Masha'Allah's work?

The reason we are informing you of the benefits of this knowledge is so that you may disseminate the correct prophecy and understanding. The alignment of the stars that resemble a placement and an achievement that you are following needs to be corrected.

What prophecy and alignment are you referring to?

> There is an experience of the star in the biblical parable of Jesus and the Three Kings. The accurate mention of the position of the luminaries in this biblical account is a tale that must be disseminated in your work if you are to achieve your goal of the ascension experience and the repair project.

NOTE: The cited parable is from the New Testament, Matthew 2: 1-12.

"After Jesus was born in Bethlehem in Judea, during the time of King Herod, Magi from the East came to Jerusalem and asked, 'Where is the one who has been born king of the Jews? We saw his star when it rose and have come to worship him'. When King Herod heard this he was disturbed, and all Jerusalem with him".

What can you tell us about this parable?

> The star is the event. The three Kings or "Magi" are the three levels of experience and the three passages of what you are calling time and time shift. The Light Body release and experience occurs in three stages and three phases. This symbolism in the story is an account that is explaining what was about to occur. This parable also contains a concealed code that relays the information about when the next experience will occur. We have already discussed the linear time frame of this event.

Are you referring to the period of 2034 to 2060?

This is when the energy begins to shift and an event that is occurring in the luminaries cannot be contained or controlled. The effect in the atmosphere and the electromagnetic experience cannot be changed or contained. This is the first experience that Man Being will be experiencing since the events recorded in the aforementioned biblical account.

The Magi brought gifts of gold, frankincense and myrrh. What do they represent in this parable?

These are codes and a description of an attempt to control the position of the satellite by absconding the resources that are required to change the electrical signal. The gold for example, has properties that allow the luminaries to remain in a somewhat stabilized position. Projects and research continues around the release of the energy through the use of gold.

What about the frankincense and myrrh?

These other properties and the examples of the objects and material that were brought are a description of the mining and the capability of the resources in the Earth plane. These materials have the ability to manifest an experience of unprecedented and unbelievable prophetic awareness. This parable describes allegorically how the luminaries are built from released energies that have been tampered with by the experiences in the Earth plane.

You're saying that we can build the Sun, Moon and stars with the release of energies from these mined materials.

> Please understand that when energy is released it does not simply coexist with other energies without contributing to an outcome. They have been created and also recreated in terms of those experiences that have been repeatedly occurring. In this case the outcome is not only the stability of the luminaries but also the building of the luminaries. The size of the physical properties of the luminaries changes according to the activity and energy that is released in the Earth plane experience.

This is enlightening.

> The interplay and the interconnection between the Earth and the Earth experience and the outlined luminaries and their existence are not an accident. This is an experience that has been created from the Earth up.

We have been taught that the solar system was formed from the collapsing of gas and dust clouds.

> The understanding that the solar system was a random event and an event of collisions and adhesions is somewhat correct but it comes from the Earth plane and continues to affect the interplay and the interconnectedness of the physical components that contain the system of your solar system and beliefs.

This begs the question - what was the purpose of our lunar missions? Were they trying to manipulate the luminosity?

Yes. They continue in their intention to try and shift the position of the luminosity. When we speak of shifting the position of the luminosity there is a way to change the way that light reaches the Earth. Once you understand that the communication and frequencies that are being released from the Earth plane and atmosphere are affecting the luminosity, you will rethink your experience in the Earth plane.

What exactly do you mean by that?

You are all being used as a mirror to project energy toward the luminaries, specifically the Moon. You are unaware of the activity in your present linear timeframe. There is an unprecedented release of energy to try to manipulate not only the Sun but also the experience of the light that is reflected back toward Earth.

Are you saying there are efforts to deprive us of the Sun and the Moon's light? Why?

The effort is in place to interfere with a signal that is coming to you from a world that you will be experiencing after the ascension event of 2034.

What specifically did they achieve with their lunar missions?

Measurements were taken of the gradient just above the surface of the Moon. The purpose was to determine what is needed to disrupt the Moon's Luminosity.

Are you saying that we're deflecting light away from Earth and from ourselves?

Yes. The Earth plane is a prison of light deficiency. This is what is keeping you immobilized.

Is this why we often associate sunny climates with happiness?

This is an accurate understanding. They are not as deficient in light.

Scientists are now telling us that the Sun is dying and will reach its end in about ten billion years.

The understanding that the Sun is dying and stars come and go is a correct understanding but the decision to allow the Sun to be destroyed is something that can be controlled and stopped. This is a plan to destroy the existence of the Beings on the planet.

What do you mean?

There will no longer be a responsibility in place for this planet once the ascension experience is completed. The mission to bring back the world that you have all been locked out of will be achieved. Once that occurs there will be no responsibility to the Earth plane of existence.

What was/is the importance of the Sirius star that we have discussed?

The Sirius star is a coordinate and there is light that once was reflected back toward your planet. This communication allowed for the assembly and the undertaking to bring back Beings. This was interfered with. The mention of Sirius in your linear accounts described a "time" where there was no longer the ability for the luminosity from the star to benefit those Beings who are in alignment with this star.

How did they interfere with Sirius?

It was much like what is being controlled in your lunar situation. The Sirius star and star system once reflected a significant amount of energy and the ability to stop this process was achieved. Once the next ascension and Messianic event of experience occurs there will be a documented history about your Moon in the same context.

Is Sirius an obsolete program? Why has there been such an emphasis placed on Sirius throughout this discussion if it no longer reflects the light?

The Beings that are organized and affiliated with Sirius are being assisted in this ascension event.

Is the Sirius star being corrected?

There is a reassembly that will once again allow certain luminaries to recalibrate and reposition themselves to effectively release the energy that is required by your Being and makeup. When this correction occurs you will innately reconnect with the luminosity and make the final correction in your ascension Light Body reassembly.

Does our Light Body reassembly create the "stars" in the sky?

You can accurately say that the stars represent a passage of time and by passage of time we refer to the passage of time through time travel and existence in Light Body and Light Body awareness. The reassembly of the Light Body and the pattern of awareness and what you are calling time travel creates an existence of a satellite.

This is complex.

Speaking about the specific physics and quantum physics and mathematics is far too advanced for your purpose in this dissemination. For now please understand that the resemblance of a star is actually a pattern of energy that exists through the experience and release of the Light Body and reassembly.

Stars are moving, even though we perceive them as being static. Is that what you mean by "resemblance of a star"?

If you consider the image of a light energy trail that follows a "comet", this is the energy that is "suspended" in a state and that you perceive as a star. By creating luminaries you are controlling the position of luminaries and affecting everything else.

After the ascension event of 2034-2060 what will become of Earth? Will there be some Beings who choose to stay?

The instability of your planet continues. There are Beings who will not choose to ascend and the instability on Earth will continue. The outrage however and questions that those Beings left behind

185

will have will instigate more knowledge and understanding about the light and the birthed light.

15

The Path of the Lyre

You've mentioned the World of Lyra and the Path of the Lyre. What exactly is this world and path?

> Lyra is an intermediary connection and world of existence. The ability to believe in Lyra and the intermediary world is more than enough for your Reader to absorb at this place and space. Lyra is equivalent to the sea of your Being. In other words you are a malleable pool of energy. Lyra is the place and space whereby you reconnect with this knowledge and form your Light Body.

Is Lyra the beginning or the end of our journey?

> Lyra is neither the beginning nor the end.

What does that mean?

> Lyra was once the beginning of your existence but is now a passageway to the unknown world that awaits your beginning in the full Light Body existence.

Why does Lyra no longer serve as our beginning? What occurred to change that?

> There was and is a split in the universe that has occurred and has allowed you to exist in a physical form and also exist in a time travel capacity allowance. Lyra is now a world of transition from your Earth density existence to your malleable Light Form embodiment. This is a discussion we will continue in another book dissemination.

Please outline the process or sequence of our ascension experience.

You will first acknowledge a shift in beliefs as you read and experience the information in this dissemination. Your belief in Lyra is the first step. That belief initializes a reconnection and a reassembly of your Light Body.

What are the following steps?

You then begin to form your Light Body over multiple stages. Once the Light Body has been assembled you will decide when you wish to "disconnect" or "release" the Light Body. This is what is called ascension. From this point you will ascend using the Iridis gateway experience. You will then rejoin the Lyra existence as a passageway through to the World of Immortality.

We pass through Lyra to another world. Is that correct?

The Lyra existence is a passageway or gateway of modification and modification of understanding. Please consider our world as a sea of information and allowance.

What is the World of Immortality?

Each of you has a world of origin. Your immortal existence is also a reconnection with your world of origin. We will further this discussion in another dialogue. Please remember that the reassembly of awareness occurs as you contain your belief in the Lyra existence.

Is there a reference to Lyra within our documented history or Bible books?

Please concern your question with the Bible Book known as Deuteronomy. Please refer specifically to the passage concerning "hearing" and "Israel" and you will understand this dialogue further. The passage is related to the Sinai experience.

NOTE: The cited passage is Deuteronomy 6: 4-9.

"Hear, O Israel. The Lord our God, the Lord is One. You shall love the Lord your God with all your heart and with all your soul and with all your might. And these words that I command you today shall be on your heart. You shall teach them diligently to your children, and shall talk of them when you sit in your house, and when you walk by the way, and when you lie down and when you rise. You shall bind them as a sign on your hand, and they shall be as frontlets between your eyes. You shall write them on the doorposts of your house and on your gates."

What is the significance of this passage?

This description is a biblical account of the attempt to retrieve the rediscovery of our world.

How is this passage about the rediscovery of Lyra?

This passage describes a call for those who can see that there is a passage of existence that provides access to Immortality. It describes the desire you all have to choose a new belief and a new design that allows the existence in the proper state of immortality and light.

Why does it read, "The Lord our God"? Has this passage also been hijacked?

"Hear the Lord, the Lord of light. The Light is One". This is what was originally communicated.

Who uttered these words?

We have said this.

What is meant by, "O Israel"? "Israel" is not a reference to a specific nation or culture of people, as we have already discussed. Is that correct?

> Israel was a term and code for those who wished to ascend and return to the gateway of the Light Body experience. It is a code for those who once again wish to reunite with the origin of their creation. These Beings are once again being asked to align their awareness. The belief that "people of Israel" are the Beings that this passage is referencing is not a correct understanding. The meaning of Israel in this passage is not related to your current cultural meaning.

Religious dogma has really twisted this.

> The confusion from the creation of the Religious Factions has created a misunderstanding about where the light goes. The light goes where it exists and the light exists in the world of Lyra. The world of Lyra is a preparation for the World of Immortality.

Going back to the vision of a light and tunnel after "death", is the light we see your world?

> Your earlier questioning about the tunnel of light and the near death experience is an accurate estimation of the experience that many of you have and will continue to have. The visualization that the light is a light from an unknown source is an inaccurate explanation. This is created by the existence of many Light Beings en masse who are present when you are making the journey through the gateway of experience.

Why then aren't we making the journey from that tunnel or gateway experience?

> Experiencing the "tunnel of light" without knowledge or preparation of ascension is the problem you are all having. There is confusion about the "near death experience" and this book can assist others in achieving an understanding. Once you place your belief in Lyra and the principles of immortality, you will follow the light. You will not choose reincarnation.

What more can you share with us about the world of Lyra?

> We have always existed for Man Being. There has always been a relationship with our world and the world you currently exist in. A decision was made to create a new civilization after the gateway had been obstructed.

Was that civilization designed to bring us home? What civilization are you referring to?

The civilization that we are referring to, you have repeatedly referred to as "Lemuria", but as we have already explained this is not the correct descriptor. Sumer is the civilization. There has been for a long time after Sumer, an obstruction in the ability to communicate with us. The communication stream has been renewed however, so that there is a new obligation for those Beings who have the ability to communicate with us to make their way to the gateway.

The communication stream is "being renewed". Does that mean we are creating the Lemuria state once again?

Yes. As we have stated there is a recall for the Lemuria experience. The gateway obstruction no longer exists in a way that has obstructed many before you.

What exactly is changing?

There is a monumental shift and those Beings that are able to make their way are doing so in this space and place. The reconnection will be creating an experience in your world where many of you will no longer choose to subscribe to the organized beliefs. The organized beliefs of Religion and the organized beliefs of Politics and the organized beliefs of Money are now concurrently shifting. This paradigm shift will create a monumental and irrevocable change in your social structure. There is a point that is being reached in your civilization and world where those that no longer subscribe to this existence will be making a radical commitment for change.

193

A Revolution?

> We are not suggesting anarchy or an overthrow. We are suggesting that many of you will no longer choose to subscribe to these paradigms. The paradigm shift will result in many of you no longer participating in the socially prescribed parameters. This will create a monumental and an irrevocable change in the structure. The ramifications are a shift in your views of Religion, Government and Money. The worldwide change that is unfolding will result in a massive instability as the power play will be reorganized.

Most people wouldn't believe this is possible.

> We are not suggesting that you will now live for free and everything will be peaceful and there will be no problems. We are suggesting that those who no longer subscribe to the light will find a huge difficulty and a lack of support.

It is difficult to imagine our World Leaders or decision makers conceding power.

> The "World Leaders" and those who are continuously guiding you away from the light will now find themselves re-circling and those who are meant to experience the light will have the experience of the re-connective ability.

Is this book an indication of a growing awareness of Lyra?

> There is a monumental change for those who are ready to make the change. The reason why we have

not been able to communicate with you until the recent dialogue is such that there is no ability for most to hear. The inability for most to hear is being corrected. The skill of listening is also being corrected. The listening stream is a series of codes and vibrations and frequencies that are foretelling a change in your civilization.

We'd like you to describe the experience of being in Lyra.

Our experience with you will be manifested in such a way that you will be feeling a physical interpretation of the communication experience. The fluidity of experience is equivalent to a swimming sea creature. This experience and ideal will further guide you along to the movement and the understanding of the movement and the listening motion. The listening motion and energy movement are equivalent capacities that you will be required to assimilate and understand.

These explanations are not easily absorbed.

Please understand this dissemination will be absorbed in stages. Your motion and your swim through the understanding of our dialogue stream will be incorporated into your Being in stages that will allow you to assimilate these ideas and undertakings further.

What do you recommend we do to help absorb these ideas?

What we are requesting is your cooperation and your communication. The communication ability lies within all of you. What we would like to remind you and your Reader of is that we belong to the light and we are from the matter that creates the reason why you seek to escape from your form of existence.

What does the name "Lyra" mean?

The place where the combined existence is realized is the unified place that we are calling "Lyra". Lyra is a word that is used to interpret the frequency of the sound that is created during the reconnection of our worlds.

Please explain what the "reconnection" is.

You are forming your Light Body. You can be in form and also be in light. This step in your ascension process is essential in that you will be growing your light embodiment and this is done in stages. As we have already stated, the next phase of the light embodiment is the release and the voluntary disconnect of the light stream.

The voluntary disconnect is a process and not a single event. Is this a correct understanding?

The voluntary disconnect is done in stages. There is not a single disconnect release. The disconnect is the release of the Light Body. The Light Body must also learn and reconnect and also proceed with a voluntary disconnect.

When you speak about the "release" of the Light Body can that also mean an expansion of form?

Yes. The word "giant" is also an accurate description in that we have the ability and awareness to contain the light and release the light when it is needed to release the light embodiment.

The word "giant" is used in our bibles and mythologies. Does this relate to your world?

There will soon be a discovery of objects that will contain an understanding about the definition and the evolution of the description of the word "giant". The fear of the giant and this cultural narrative further perpetuates the understanding that the release of the light and the release of the awareness is not something that is to be expected or beneficial. Doing away with the negative connotation of the term "giant" will be of benefit to your Reader.

We created legends about man-eating giants to deter us from light expansion. Is that what you're saying?

This is somewhat accurate. Understand that the concept or definition of "giant" is a description that pertains to a Being of unlimited height of awareness and connectivity. This lack of confinement allows the mobility and the time travel modality to function.

We are finally releasing ourselves from this confinement.

You are speeding up the existence of the light cells and the first stage of the voluntary disconnect involves an elevated experience of form.

It sounds like we are becoming giants.

There is some truth in this assessment. You are embodying the understandings that will allow you to release yourselves in the voluntary disconnect and reform into an elevated Light Body. The elevated Light Body is now something you can choose and continue to form an understanding about.

Is there one final message you'd like to end this volume with?

Yes. There will be a discovery of a disseminated work that has been forgotten. This will create a general interest among those you identify as "unbelievers".

What is the discovery?

It is a book. This book is key to reestablishing the understanding that our world is in existence and an important aspect of all of your belief streams. The book is not a book that you will be purchasing. It is a book that has an accounting and the accounting is a recount and request for those Beings who wish to make ascension. The book has been created in an allegorical style and many of you may not recognize the understanding. This book is of key importance as there has not been anything like this discovered in the area that it will be discovered in. It is not necessarily an intact book but understand that it is a record and the record itself may explain the existence of the book in question. This book is not known and has been forgotten. There has been a concerted effort to hide this information and the information has been lost to the awareness of the Abrahamic religions. This discovery is something that connects all the religions and also makes known the Akhenaten story.

We will pay attention to the recovery of artifacts and continue this connection.

Our final recommendation is to read and reread this material and allow the absorption to occur. Our reconnection and discussion continues.

CLOSING MESSAGE *from Lyra Beings*

We have discussed a lot about what Man Being is lacking in this dialogue. We do however admire your attempts to correct your situation. There have been many attempts. There have been many positive contributions but there are also those who are perpetuating the problem unknowingly by espousing seemingly positive ideals that keep you all bound to your consumptive and unhappy existence.

We admire that some of you do not seem to give up and keep trying to find a solution. This may not always be efficient but we admire that some of you are committed to the cause to try and repair things. We also admire that some of you are broadcasting and disseminating information albeit this is not always received in a serious fashion. If we felt that this situation was not fixable then we would abandon this project entirely. The truth of the situation is that when you realize what the condition is, you will be willing to further commit to the Repair Project.

When you manifest a modification ultimately this will improve conditions for further modification. Communication improves and as more Beings engage in a unified dialogue then what you term a "call to arms" will take place. We would like to support all of you in your ascension process. Once there is a substantial improved awareness for all, then the conditions will improve automatically. You will be generating a signal and a frequency in tandem. This is not a singular activity and requires a monumental effort to generate a strong frequency and a signal.

This is a group effort and you must call each other to awareness. Things will automatically resolve themselves once there is a stronger signal. You will emit a frequency collectively. This is what is needed to improve the condition. Once the signal is manifested then further transmission and instructions will be absorbed. New energy frequency exchanges resonance through intracellular transmission instruction. This is a code you will soon decipher.

Printed in Great Britain
by Amazon

20791138R00123